A LITTLE BOOK

FOR NEW

BIBLE SCHOLARS

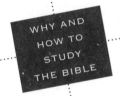

WHY AND
HOW TO
STUDY
THE BIBLE

E. RANDOLPH RICHARDS
& JOSEPH R. DODSON

D0366271

IVP Academic

An imprint of InterVarsity Press
Downers Grove, Illinois

InterVarsity Press
P.O. Box 1400, Downers Grove, IL 60515-1426
ivpress.com
email@ivpress.com

*InterVarsity Press® is the book-publishing division of InterVarsity Christian Fellowship/USA®,
a movement of students and faculty active on campus at hundreds of universities, colleges, and
schools of nursing in the United States of America, and a member movement of the
International Fellowship of Evangelical Students. For information about local and regional
activities, visit intervarsity.org.*

*All Scripture quotations, unless otherwise indicated, are taken from THE HOLY BIBLE, NEW
INTERNATIONAL VERSION®, NIV® Copyright © 1973, 1978, 1984, 2011 by Biblica, Inc.™
Used by permission. All rights reserved worldwide.*

*While any stories in this book are true, some names and identifying information may have
been changed to protect the privacy of individuals.*

*Digitized image of Papyrus 46 used by permission of The Center for the Study of New
Testament Manuscripts at the University of Michigan, www.csntm.org.*

Cover design: Cindy Kiple
Interior design: Beth McGill

ISBN 978-0-8308-5170-6 (print)
ISBN 978-0-8308-8305-9 (digital)

Printed in the United States of America ♾

Library of Congress Cataloging-in-Publication Data
*Names: Richards, E. Randolph (Ernest Randolph), author. | Dodson, Joseph R.,
  author.*
*Title: A little book for new Bible scholars / E. Randolph Richards and Joseph
  R. Dodson.*
*Description: Downers Grove, IL : InterVarsity Press, 2017. | Includes
  bibliographical references and index.*
*Identifiers: LCCN 2017000161 (print) | LCCN 2017000760 (ebook) | ISBN
  9780830851706 (pbk. : alk. paper) | ISBN 9780830883059 (eBook)*
Subjects: LCSH: Bible--Study and teaching.
*Classification: LCC BS600.3 .R53 2017 (print) | LCC BS600.3 (ebook) | DDC
  220.07--dc23*
LC record available at https://lccn.loc.gov/2017000161

P	18	17	16	15	14	13	12	11	10	9	8	7	6	5	4	3	2	1
Y	32	31	30	29	28	27	26	25	24	23	22	21	20	19	18	17		

"A delightful read and absolutely on target, *A Little Book for New Bible Scholars* gets my highest praise and recommendation. It should be required reading early in the program for all students preparing for ministry."

J. Daniel Hays, Ouachita Baptist University

"Plotting a course of study or even a career in biblical studies can be fraught with many trials and temptations. In this charming little book, Joey Dodson and Randy Richards offer some sage advice to budding students of the Bible on how to keep their egos intact, how to keep their faith authentic, how to use their vat of new biblical knowledge to serve others, and how to grow as Christians through biblical studies. Everyone should read this book before seminary!"

Michael F. Bird, lecturer in theology, Ridley College, Melbourne, Australia

"This delightful volume is full of wit and wisdom not only for biblical scholars and theologians but for all students of the Word. The stories, anecdotes, and insights will encourage you to discover more deeply the riches of God's Word and the heart of Christian ministry."

Mark L. Strauss, university professor of New Testament, Bethel Seminary San Diego

"Dodson and Richards have given young biblical scholars a book that charms while it instructs. Their combined years of wisdom are presented with whimsy and honesty that will be helpful in discernment for emerging biblical scholars. This book gets at not only the head knowledge, but also the heart. The interspersing of other biblical scholars throughout the book adds diversity, breadth, and weight to each chapter. As an advisor for students pursuing work in biblical scholarship as their vocation, this is precisely the kind of book I will gladly recommend to them!"

Beth M. Stovell, assistant professor of Old Testament, Ambrose Seminary

"Richards and Dodson give us all a profound gift, shining light on the 'narrow way' to sweet satisfaction in biblical scholarship. It is found not in exploiting a career for personal gain, social approval, or vanity, but in enjoying the riches of God's Word among God's people. This is a rich store of wisdom."

Timothy Gombis, professor of New Testament, Grand Rapids Theological Seminary

"*A Little Book for New Bible Scholars* is a fun and challenging look at the joys and realities of the academic study of the Bible. Richards and Dodson offer wise yet practical advice, peppered with words of warning, about studying the Bible academically. Not only is their advice for new scholars, it is also full of valuable reminders about the benefits and pitfalls of biblical learning for those of us who are no longer beginners."

Benjamin E. Reynolds, associate professor of New Testament, Tyndale University College, Toronto

"Whether starting out in formal biblical studies as a freshman at a Christian college or completing a PhD in Old or New Testament, students of the Bible need to read this little gem of a book. A veteran biblical scholar joins hands with a younger peer to offer all the right advice about how to approach one's career, what to avoid, and how to keep the main thing the main thing. Laced with humorous and incisive real-life stories and choice quotes from other scholars who have trodden the same path, this work represents Christian wisdom at its finest."

Craig L. Blomberg, distinguished professor of New Testament, Denver Seminary

"To snorkel or to dive? That is the question this little book asks its readers to consider. In a well-written and personally engaging reflection on the vocation of biblical studies, Richards, Dodson, and a collection of scholars invite would-be Bible students to consider anew the importance of the discipline of academic Bible study for the benefit of both one's personal life and the ministry of the church. The church of our time is desperate for the pastor-theologian who has the skill and the theologically chastened intuition to wrestle with the significant challenges of a twenty-first-century world with its lightning-fast revolutions in science, sexuality, and globalization—to name just a few. This kind of leader is increasingly becoming the most significant commodity for the twenty-first-century church. The authors are seasoned guides as well as cheerleaders for a new generation of lifelong students of Scripture for the sake of the Messiah Jesus' church."

Joel Willitts, professor of biblical and theological studies, North Park University

CONTENTS

PREFACE

■ ■ ■

ONE DAY AFTER CLASS MY PROFESSOR, Calvin Miller, remarked, "Joey, we are a product of our teachers' teachers. Like those who have gone before you, don't just bear fruit. Bear fruit trees!"

Although we, Randy and Joey, come from different generations and different educational paths, we both see our professors' influence all over our lives. We are forever grateful to the men and women who were faithful to pass along to us what they received from their teachers, and we've done our best to follow their example. Randy has done so since 1988 by teaching at evangelical institutions in Texas, Indonesia, Arkansas, and now, Florida. Joey has been teaching since 2005 in universities in Texas, Scotland, and Arkansas. This little book is a modest attempt to give back by sharing from the overflow of what we've learned. We aim to help prepare the next generation of "fruit trees"—those who will be Bible teachers after us.

In writing this book, we thought about the things we routinely tell our own students who are new Bible scholars. We also asked other well-respected Bible scholars what kinds of things they routinely tell their students. We included many stories—true, personal stories. They're written in the first person and use "I," but we wanted to avoid muddying the waters by constantly indicating who the "I" is. When it matters, such as when the story is about our particular families, we found a way to weave in who's talking. This book, though, isn't about us; it's about you. We wrote for the man or woman who is embarking on a program in biblical studies. Although this usually means a college major or minor or the standard entry track in seminary, some churches are engaging in quality, in-depth biblical training for select leaders. Whatever your path into biblical studies and whatever your goal, we pray God's richest blessings on your studies.

Joey would like to thank Ouachita Baptist University for granting him a sabbatical to work on this project, as well as the faculty and staff of Southeastern Baptist Theological Seminary for sharing their resources during the sabbatical. Randy thanks Palm Beach Atlantic University for valuing scholarship and allowing him to carve out time for it. We are both indebted to the professors who graciously volunteered testimonials for this book. We also need to thank Brandon O'Brien, a wonderful writer, friend, and Bible scholar, for his insightful comments on the book. Although we dedicate this book to all our students, we especially note L. J. Brooks, Joey's son in the faith, who aced life's final exam in 2012.

INTRODUCTION

A Noble Calling

■ ■ ■

ONE DAY WHEN I WAS READING REVELATION, I came across a passage where John recounts his heavenly vision:

> Then I saw in the right hand of him who sat on the throne a scroll with writing on both sides and sealed with seven seals. And I saw a mighty angel proclaiming in a loud voice, "Who is worthy to break the seals and open the scroll?" (Rev 5:1-2)

Although I had planned to read the rest of Revelation that day, my curiosity got the best of me. I was puzzled. Why would a scroll have seven seals? At first blush, I guessed that seven seals likely meant "sealed really well." Then I thought that seven seals could imply "spiritually sealed." Finally, rather than just sitting there and pondering it, I thought, *I should research this.* So I did. And here's what I found.

My initial interpretations were way off. A person hearing this story in the first century would have thought, *Seven seals? Oh, that's a will,* as in a "last will and testament." You see, in the Roman Empire, an ordinary person would gather the heir of the will, the executor, and five witnesses to hear him dictate his will to a secretary. When the document was finished, it was rolled up. Each person attested that it was correct and made it official by wrapping a string around it, tying it up, putting a blob of clay or wax on his knot, and then pressing his seal into the wax. Thus, the will would have seven seals.[1]

It's very exciting to think of the implications of Revelation 5 from this perspective. Since the setting in Revelation is a heavenly throne scene, the will with seven seals is the will and testament of God the Father! Moreover, John lets the reader know that this is not a little will. He says that when it was rolled up, one could see the scroll was written on both sides, indicating that the entire document was full of text. In other words, this will has a lot of stuff in it. It's unsurprising that all of heaven is chomping at the bit to find out what it says.

There's a problem, however. The will is sealed, and "no one in heaven or on earth or under the earth could open the scroll or even look inside it" (Rev 5:3). Not a single creature in heaven or on earth or under the earth was worthy to break the seals. Not even among the innumerable angels, or the six-winged seraphim

---

[1]When it was time to make the inheritance official, the heir and the executor had to be there along with a majority of the witnesses. A papyrus from AD 325 actually describes the opening of a will:

The executor says to the secretary, "In the presence of whom did you make out the will?"

The notary answers, "The signatories."

The executor asks, "How many signatories are there?"

The notary answers, "Seven, and four are present."

The executor says, "Let the four subscribe that they have recognized their own seals."

After the signatories present had subscribed that they recognized their own seals, the will was opened and read.

(Isa 6:2), or the crown-wearing elders (Rev 4:4). None of the seals belonged to them. Not one had been there when the will was written and sealed.

In response, John wails and sobs because none of the seven were there to open the will.[2] But then someone comes forward. John's eyes behold a lamb "looking as if it had been slain, standing at the center of the throne" (Rev 5:6). It is Jesus! Jesus steps up, takes the will from the Father, and opens all seven seals.

This is the part we are supposed to notice. His authority to open all the seals reveals that Jesus is the executor of the will. More than that, however, he is also all five witnesses. Since there had been no one else to witness it but Christ, this will must have been written before creation—before anyone else was around. What is more, in addition to being the executor and witness of the will, he is the heir. Jesus is the Son of God who will inherit it all. As the hosts of angels go on to broadcast, Jesus will receive "power and wealth and wisdom and strength and honor and glory and praise!" (Rev 5:12).

If you love learning about how the first century background illumines passages like this, then deeper Bible study is for you. While we acknowledge that the truth of God's Word is radically simple, transforming, and true, we also maintain that Scripture was carefully constructed and is profoundly complex. The same God whose creation is marvelously wonderful and diverse gave us his Word, which, though simple and clear, has sophisticated depth and richness for us to discover.

---

[2]We might seem a bit dramatic here, but the original Greek text uses a verb that stresses how John continued to weep and follows it with the adjective translated as "much" to emphasize how profusely he cried.

Early in my Christian journey, I recognized that the Bible is the inspired word of God—the very words of our Creator. At the same time I was in awe of the majesty of God splashed all over creation. *God spoke all of this into existence.* I put two and two together and thought, *If the God who spoke this universe into existence also spoke the Scriptures into existence, then I want to give my life to studying these words.* Pursuing biblical studies has been both an adventure and a dream. Engaging God's living word—and letting him engage me—has been the most life-giving vocation I could ever imagine.

Preston Sprinkle, New Testament scholar

When the Richards boys were teenagers, I took them to Blanchard Springs Caverns in the Ozark Mountains and signed us up for the "wild cave tour." Before we departed for the caves, the guides made sure we would be able to crawl on our bellies, tolerate tight spaces, and be willing to get dirty from head to toe. They had us sign waivers assuring them that we realized we were taking our lives into our own hands. Then they issued special equipment and introduced us to our personal guide. For the rest of the day, we crawled through tiny holes. We inched along a ledge with our backs against one wall, our legs braced against the other, and a gorge underneath us. We skirted other dangerous areas. If our headlamps gave out, we would be in deepest darkness. There were no paths and no ropes to mark the walkways. We ate our sack lunches in some deep cavern and then began our ascent. After crawling through a narrow—really narrow—tube, we squeezed through a crevice and emerged on the path of the standard tour, just behind the ropes. Imagine the surprise of the regular tourists when these four bedraggled folks, who seemed to materialize out of a crack, stood up and stepped across the rope and onto the guided path. We were covered with dirt, sweat, and smiles. To be sure, our journey wasn't for everyone. Most people couldn't take the claustrophobic spaces. We certainly got our hands (and every other inch of us) dirty. But to see certain treasures required the hard work.

The same is true of advanced biblical studies. Those willing to don the equipment, turn on their headlamps and head underground into dark caves of vocabulary and ancient philosophy—those willing to inch through tubes of church tradition and theology—those willing to brave narrow places recently discovered and to skirt dangerous areas still waiting to be explored—will find untold riches.

This little book is written for those who desire to go beyond the beaten path to pursue biblical studies, whether it is in college, seminary, or an advanced church program. We hope to show you that biblical studies is a noble calling—that it can enable you all the more to act justly, to love mercy, and to walk humbly before the Lord. Moreover, we want to show you that biblical studies can help us understand the gospel of Jesus Christ more fully so that we can teach it in our churches more effectively. We should warn you, however, that while graduating college with a major in chemistry makes you a chemist and finishing a major in engineering makes you an engineer, completing a major in biblical studies makes you not so much a Bible *expert* as much as a lifelong Bible *student*. We chafe at part of our book's title—Bible *Scholars*—but we didn't know how else to term it. Even though both of your authors have completed PhDs in biblical studies, we remain always and forever *students* of the Bible. There is so much yet to learn and we have an ever-increasing hunger to learn it, not to mention a matching desire to see it faithfully applied to our lives and churches.

1

FALL IN LOVE

■■■

I MET HER WHEN I WAS IN FIRST GRADE. She walked into the cafeteria as I was sipping chocolate milk and munching tater tots. I was so compelled by her beauty, I pushed away my tray, stood on my chair, and shouted, "Who is *that* pretty girl?!" Although I'm not certain I believe in love at first sight, we've been together ever since. I pursued her throughout elementary school and declared my love in sixth grade by stealing a kiss (a romantic peck on the cheek). In junior high, I had not yet hit my growth spurt, so at the homecoming dance I was forced to put my head on *her* shoulder as we swayed the night away. In high school, we went on our first mission trip together, where we both surrendered to the ministry. As I fell in deeper love with her throughout the ensuing years, I wanted to know every detail I could about her. And the more I learned about her, the more I fell in love with her. Now, twenty years of marriage and five little Dodsons later, I am still tempted to stand up whenever she walks into the room.

I also met Jesus Christ as my Savior when I was in first grade. I stood up from my pew, walked down the aisle and declared my commitment to God. The next Sunday, I made it official by following the Lord in baptism. To congratulate me, the church gave me a black, leather-bound, red-letter edition Bible with my name engraved on the front. The more I grew in my relationship with God, the more I wanted to tuck into that Bible. And the more I read that Bible, the more I grew in my relationship with God. My zeal for the Lord and his Word led me to a Christian liberal arts university where I began my education in biblical studies. Even after a handful of degrees and decades in a classroom, I continue to be amazed at how God constantly opens my eyes to wonderful things in his Word—insights that I have never seen before (Ps 119:18). My love for the Lord has motivated me to study the Bible all the more.

IS LOVE ALL I NEED?

As much as I had love for the Lord, I needed something else. Against the popular sentiment that in the Christian life all you need is love, Scripture makes it clear that love is *not* all you need. Yes, love for God is paramount and essential (Deut 6:5). But in Philippians 1:9-11, Paul demonstrates the need for knowledge in addition to love. In the passage, Paul tells the church that he is constantly praying that their love will continue to increase more and more in all knowledge and insight. Elsewhere Paul warns of the dangers of having knowledge without love: knowledge puffs us up and leads to pride (1 Cor 8:1), and even a person smart enough to fathom every cosmic mystery is nothing without love (1 Cor 13:1-2). This does not mean that Paul wants his people to be ignorant. Just as we should avoid knowledge without love, we should also avoid love without knowledge. Paul prays that his church will have both. As Warren Wiersbe wrote, "Christian love is not blind! The heart and mind work together so that we have discerning love and loving discernment."[1]

Similarly, Peter commands the church to make every effort to add knowledge to their faith, since knowledge is necessary for preventing believers from becoming spiritually blind (2 Pet 1:5-9). Furthermore, what I've realized throughout the years is that the knowledge I need goes beyond simply knowing what the Bible says—it's the knowledge necessary to correctly handle the Bible and interpret what it says.

IS THE BIBLE ALL I NEED?

A popular Christian speaker asked the question "If I were on an island, and I only had the Bible—no one preaching to me, no theology books—what would I believe?" This is an interesting question, but it can imply that a person would not need anything but a Bible to understand the Bible. To be sure, studying *about* the Bible can never replace studying Scripture. Nevertheless, there is more to understanding Scripture than just reading the Bible. In fact, if all you had were the Bible, you would have something that looks like the figure on the next page.

That is to say, the only reason we have an English Bible (or even a printed Greek text) is because of the hard work of biblical scholars who were not alone on an island. It took centuries of work by innumerable scholars to enable us to hold a modern Bible in our hand. Assuming someone has already translated Scripture into English, is my English Bible enough? Alone on an island, I would not have a community of believers around me nor

---

[1]Warren W. Wiersbe, *Be Joyful* (Wheaton, IL: Victor Books, 1974), 26.

Sample from a late second- or early third-century papyrus of Paul's letters (P46).

the great cloud of witnesses who came before me to check, confirm, or complement my interpretations.[2] I might discard the Bible as contradicting itself when I read, "Do not answer a fool according to his folly" and then see in the next verse, "Answer a fool according to his folly" (Prov 26:4-5). I'd be puzzled by how Moses could write about himself in Numbers 12:3, "Now Moses was a very humble man, more humble than anyone else on the face of the earth." Isn't it haughty to call yourself humble? Moreover, I'd probably believe in baptism for the dead (1 Cor 15:29), snake handling (Mk 16:18), and polygamy (1 Sam 1:2). I might be against women wearing pearl jewelry (1 Tim 2:9), and think it is okay for someone to dress like a prostitute to seduce her father-in-law (Gen 38). I'd possibly conclude that pressing a child's foreskin to his father's heel turns away God's wrath (Ex 4:24-26) or that I should pray for God to bash the heads of my enemies' babies against a rock (Ps 137:9).

As history has shown us, when a person just "reads their Bible," the result can be bad theology the likes of which has been used to support slavery, bully women, and spread heresies about Christ.[3] In the 1990s, among a cluster of islands in eastern Indonesia, a "new biblical insight" arose. Some pastors had been diligently studying their Bibles—a good thing to do. They noticed that at Jesus' baptism God had announced, "This is my Son" (Mt 3:17). Then at Jesus' crucifixion, Jesus exclaims, "My God, my God, why have you forsaken me?" (Mt 27:46). Those Indonesian

---

[2]Cf. Scot McKnight, *The King Jesus Gospel* (Grand Rapids: Zondervan, 2011).
[3]We don't think the Bible supports slavery, women-hating, or gay-bashing; see E. Randolph Richards and Brandon J. O'Brien, *Paul Behaving Badly* (Downers Grove, IL: InterVarsity Press, 2016).

pastors "discovered" the idea that the human Jesus became the Son of God when God adopted him at his baptism and then un-adopted him at his crucifixion, so that only the human Jesus died on the cross. This idea spread like wildfire across a dozen islands and hundreds of churches. Then someone on the mission board said, "Hey, let's dispatch that rookie, Randy, to address it." At that point, I was glad I had read more than just my Bible. Having studied theology and church history, I recognized that this was just the old adoptionist heresy. I had both the biblical and historical training to help untangle the mess. I detailed how the church, with its apostolic, rule-of-faith-shaped way of reading Scripture, had already responded to and rejected this heresy, and why their decision still applies today.[4]

Being alone on an island with just my Bible could not only lead me—like those Indonesian pastors—to biblical errors and fallacies, but it would also hinder me from understanding Scripture more fully. For example, if I just "read my Bible," I might miss how decisively Genesis 1 turns other ancient cosmologies on their heads. I might not get what is funny about Gideon threshing wheat *in a valley*. I'd probably not notice how Luke cleverly hints at the trial of Socrates when Paul stands before the philosophers on Mars Hill in Acts 17, and I'd certainly miss the significance of that allusion. These are all things that the original audience would have understood better than we do when we just "read the Bible."

---

[4]It is frequently noted that "those that fail to learn from history, are doomed to repeat it." It may be even truer of church history. Cf. Matthew W. Bates, *The Hermeneutics of the Apostolic Proclamation* (Waco, TX: Baylor University Press, 2012).

Take 1 Corinthians 13:1-3, for instance, where Paul states that love is the key to ministry. If I only had an English Bible without the help of scholarly commentary, I would not know that the translators of my Bible had to decide whether Paul wrote, "If I give all I possess to the poor and give over my body *to hardship that I may boast*, but do not have love, I gain nothing," or whether he wrote "If I give all I possess to the poor and give over my body *to be burned*, but do not have love, I gain nothing." The difference in the Greek text is a single letter in the middle of a word: ΚΑΥΞΗΣΩΜΑΙ vs. ΚΑΥΘΗΣΩΜΑΙ. Not much of a difference! I would also not know whether Paul meant that those without love are like "clanging metal *or* cymbals," or if he meant that those without love are like "clanging metal *rather than* resonate cymbals." You see, the single-letter word ἤ that separates *metal* from *cymbals* can be translated "or," but it can also be translated as "rather than." A number of translations go with the first interpretation so that they render the word *chalkos*, "brass" or "bronze," as "gong." But Paul never actually wrote "gong." Translators guessed that since Paul wrote cymbals, he must have meant a gong when he wrote *chalkos*, "bronze." But it seems more likely that Paul meant just a piece of bronze rather than a musical instrument.[5] Similarly, Paul likely intended to say that if someone teaches without love, the basic material (the "bronze") may be there but their teaching will clack like a loud lump of *chalkia* rather than ringing beautifully like a cymbal.[6] Of course,

---

[5]Plato once quipped that some orators won't shut up; they are like *chalkia* ("bronze things") that "ring a long time after they have been struck." Plato, *Protagoras* 329a (W. R. M. Lamb, LCL), 153.

[6]Todd K. Sanders, "A New Approach to 1 Corinthians 13.1," *NTS* 36 (1990): 614-18, esp. 616.

it is perfectly fine simply to enjoy the beautiful passage on love. But if you are willing to come off the island and read more than just the Bible, a more in-depth look reveals two different translation/interpretation challenges that come down to an issue of a single Greek letter.

> I was sitting in Charlie (C. F. D.) Moule's little flat in my first term at Cambridge, discussing with him an essay he'd asked me to write. I was sure some of the scholars one book was citing were mistaken, and I wanted to understand why. There began my journey. Until that time, I knew the Bible was a wonderful resource for living the Christian life. Now I also understood that there was a depth to engaging intellectually with it that was worthwhile (for the Bible, rightly interpreted, feeds the life of the church) and challenging (and so worth devoting my life to).
>
> Steve Walton, New Testament scholar

CONCLUSION

The field of biblical studies reminds me that I am always only sometimes right. This is the case because, as John Walton reminds us, even though the Bible was written *for* us (and for all humanity), it was not written *to* us.[7] We come to the text with Western lenses and modern baggage. Because of the cultural distance that stands between us and the Bible, our field takes seriously the task of bridging the gap by analyzing what the

---

[7]John Walton, *The Lost World of Genesis One: Ancient Cosmology and the Origins Debate* (Downers Grove, IL: InterVarsity Press, 2009), 9.

biblical text says, what it means, and how it is best applied. To borrow from Dietrich Bonhoeffer, biblical studies teaches us how to read the Bible over against ourselves before we try to read it for ourselves.

Anti-intellectual Christians may be afraid of analyzing the Bible critically for fear that what they discover will invalidate Scripture. They rush to rescue the Bible from honest examination and instead push their interpretations without question. But just as Socrates said that the unexamined life is not worth living, we believe the unexamined faith is not worth having. As for me, I have tested Scripture in pursuit of the truth, and it has always faithfully led me back to the reliability of the Bible—even if it sometimes leads me away from some previously held interpretation. As a result of biblical studies, my trust in the Lord and his Word is worth more than it has ever been before. To be sure, by the grace of God, I've come a long way from chocolate milk and tater tots, but my love for the Lord still drives me to study the Bible. Now, however, I do so with better tools to enhance my understanding of Scripture and with the help of other scholars to help me avoid misinterpreting it. Our churches today are full of thoughtful and curious Christians who love God and his Word, and who desire ministers who can teach Scripture well.

MORE STUFF,
LESS FLUFF

■■■

WHEN I WAS A SOPHOMORE IN COLLEGE, my Bible professor, J. Scott Duvall, had the keen insight to discern that I was mostly show. I was a flamboyant youth communicator and thought highly of my homiletic skills. After all, weren't youth coming to know the Lord through my sermons? Dr. Duvall kindly noted, "Joey, you have *noise*, but biblical studies will give you *volume*." What he meant was that although I had enough knowledge to lead students to Christ, I did not have enough to take them much further. I had panache to make converts but lacked the training needed to make disciples. I came to realize that to do the latter I needed more than a handful of Bible verses and a knack for entertaining audiences. I needed less fluff and more stuff.

BE AN OWL, NOT A PEACOCK

The ancient philosopher Dio complained similarly about the popular orators of his day.[1] They too were more fluff than stuff.

---

[1] Dio Chrysostom, *On Man's First Conception of God* 1-6.

According to Dio, they strutted around like peacocks to impress their audience with the plumage of their many-colored, fancy words. But Dio insisted that humanity needs owls, not peacocks. He admitted that an owl may appear insignificant and weak in comparison to a peacock, and that her song may not be as pleasing as a nightingale, but—in Dio's illustration—when an owl speaks, she speaks divine words of wisdom. While peacocks use ear-tickling platitudes to draw people to themselves, Dio concluded that owls use plain speech to draw people to truth.

These "peacocks" also strutted around the cities where Paul ministered. In fact, there was a group of them in Corinth. Similar to Dio, Paul refused to be like the eloquent preachers of his day. Instead, as he stressed in 1 Corinthians, he was sent "to preach the gospel—not with wisdom and eloquence" (1 Cor 1:17). Rather than hiding his weaknesses and coming to the Corinthians with clever words, the apostle preached the Word of God to them in spiritual power. As a result, their faith rested not on human wisdom but on divine authority (1 Cor 2:1-5). Paul didn't just avoid fluff; he gave them stuff. He wove sophisticated arguments with Old Testament passages and counted on his audience being biblically literate enough to follow his point.

BEYOND THE BASICS, PLEASE

Studying the Bible assists us in helping others beyond the basics of the gospel. Although Paul resolved only to know Christ and Christ crucified when he shared the gospel with the Corinthians, he did not stop there. Sure, Paul had given the believers spiritual milk at first. As infants in Christ, that's all they could handle at the time. In 1 Corinthians 3:2, however, Paul vents his frustration that they are not ready to move beyond the basics: "I gave you milk, not solid food, for you were not yet ready for it." He goes on to bemoan, "Indeed, you are still not ready." His letters to the church show his effort in biblical studies to feed the believers some solid exegetical fare.

The author of Hebrews expressed the same complaint with his audience. He urges the church to move beyond the elementary teachings—the ABCs—about Christ. He is ready to take his congregation forward to maturity and he expresses the familiar frustration, "You need milk, not solid food!" Because they were still more fluff than stuff, he chides: "In fact, though by this time you ought to be teachers, you need someone to teach you the elementary truths of God's word all over again." (Heb 5:12). It's as if the author is asking the believers, "How can you guide people to a place where you have not yet been?" We should ask ourselves the same question. We cannot take people beyond the basics if we ourselves have not yet studied beyond them.

Take the story of the widow's offering in Luke 21. It's another example in Luke's Gospel of Jesus using a teachable moment with his disciples to make a wonderful point:

> As Jesus looked up, he saw the rich putting their gifts into the temple treasury. He also saw a poor widow put in two very small copper coins [mites]. "Truly I tell you," he said, "this poor widow has put in more than all the others. All these people gave their gifts out of their wealth; but she out of her poverty put in all she had to live on." (Lk 21:1-4)

Growing up I heard many a message from this beautiful story, usually exhorting our little church to give above and beyond. A campaign for a major remodel could scarcely be done without several references to the widow's sacrificial giving. While the story underlines Jesus' simple and marvelous message that God looks at the giver's heart and not at the amount of the gift, the context of the story also offers a subtle warning to religious leaders that most readers miss.

First, look at the passage that comes just before the story of the widow's gift (Lk 20:45-47). There Jesus warns his audience to watch out for the religious leaders who devour *widows'* houses (Lk 20:47). These high and mighty teachers who prayed long prayers and walked around in flowing robes would stoop so low as to seize a widow's house if she could not pay her debts.[2] A widow with no money could be turned out on the street. And in the very next story, we read about a widow who gave her last two coins to the temple. Wait, you say, surely this is different; the gift was to the temple. But look at what Jesus says in verse 6 immediately following the story of the widow: the temple is beautiful but it will be destroyed (Lk 21:5-6).

By stacking these three stories one after another—devouring widows' houses (20:47), the widow's gift to the temple (21:1-4), and the temple's destruction (21:5-6)—Luke was adding a second, subtle, warning. Religious leaders can use a person's devotion to squeeze out money that the person cannot really afford. Here's a widow who gave her last coins to the temple and the temple isn't even going to last. Be careful, religious leaders, that you don't use someone's piety to squeeze every last dime out of them. Yikes! When I was growing up in church, that was exactly

---

[2]Cf. Matthew 18:25.

what the story of the widow's coins was used for: to push the devout into giving more money. Obviously, we don't want to miss the simple and beautiful point that Jesus made to his disciples: God looks at the heart of the giver and not the size of the gift. But are we off the hook if we've never noticed Luke's warning to religious leaders? Since we are admonished to handle accurately the word of truth (2 Tim 2:15), I think not. God expects us to move beyond milk to serious meat so that we can be mature teachers of his Word.

A Bible study leader should teach more than brow-wrinkling fluff and threadbare applications. She should offer serious content to those hungry to know and apply God's Word. Moreover, we need to teach more than just our canon within a canon (meaning just our favorite book or books). But, as mentioned above, we can't take others where we haven't been.

During my first year of seminary I was not very impressed with the level of biblical scholarship I encountered. There seemed to be little robust critical thinking going on. Then I took a course in hermeneutics. This professor challenged us never to settle for mediocrity or the status quo. "Christians," he said, "should be the very best in their field. They should be the best scientists, the best archaeologists, the best linguists, the best historians. We are not here simply to defend our beliefs. We are here to seek truth." That course and those words set me on a course of a lifetime of biblical scholarship.

Mark L. Strauss, New Testament scholar

BUILD A STRONG FOUNDATION

I called one of my mentors before I left for Scotland to get some words of wisdom. He said, "Joey, don't just order from one section of the menu." What he meant was that since I loved the New Testament and especially enjoyed concentrating on the writings of Paul, it would be easy for me to marginalize other sections of the Bible. I had a tendency to get lost in Paul's letters, and even when I did venture outside of them, I did not tend to go into the Old Testament as often as I should have. There is a real danger when young scholars concentrate on one area of the Bible too soon. Beginning biblical studies should be like pouring concrete for a foundation. You want a large, strong foundation. The Bible is a big book. Actually, in a sense, it's a library of over sixty books. You need to be acquainted with all of it. That's an intimidating task.

When I walk into a library, I'm often overwhelmed by the feeling that *every* book around me represents something I don't know. There's a flood of publications about every book of the Bible. It's not just the biblical books but even individual verses in those books that receive volumes of scholarly attention, such as an entire book on half a verse in Leviticus.[3] Consequently, just keeping up with research surrounding a book like Romans— much less on all of Paul—often seems like a herculean task. It isn't even possible to *read* all the new books on Paul. It's daunting and even a bit depressing. What is a beginning Bible scholar to do when such a tsunami of books looms? You need a guide.

---

[3]Leviticus 18:5b; see the excellent work by Preston Sprinkle, *Law and Life*, WUNT (Tübingen: Mohr Siebeck, 2007).

Your instructors or mentors will steer you toward the most essential books and articles. While you may think when you look at their syllabi that they are asking you to read *everything*, they have in fact whittled it down to the bare essentials. This is why professors insist you read what is assigned. Why pay for an education and then not get it? That would be like ordering food and then not eating it.

CONCLUSION: STUFF NOT FLUFF CREATES THE OVERFLOW

When I was in college one of the most humble and godly men in my hometown passed away. A few days before he died, hospice nurses came to his house to give him medicine to help him with the pain. The nurses warned his wife that the particular drugs would likely cause him to lose control of his mental capacity so that whatever was in his heart was going to come out without a filter. She needed to brace herself for prideful words, angry outbursts, and crude comments. The nurses dosed him up, and as they expected for the last hours of his life what was in his heart and mind freely gushed out. What he said, however, was not rude or uncouth. Rather, for the last hours of his life, all he did was quote Scripture! The final words on his lips were from the overflow of his heart: his inner conversation was replete with God's Word. Since that day I've prayed that I would fill my heart with Scripture so that if I am ever put into that position, rather than spewing forth inappropriate words that make my family cringe, my final words would be a melody of Scripture to encourage them. I'm convinced that only a life committed to studying stuff not fluff can enable me to do so.

3

HOLD YOUR HORSES!

■ ■ ■

THERE IS A BEAUTIFUL proverb in Scripture:

> The horse is made ready for the day of battle,
> but victory rests with the LORD. (Prov 21:31)

Although the main point of this proverb is that victory belongs to the Lord, we should not overlook the obvious—what nearly went without being said—"the horse is made ready for the day of battle." Victory belongs to the Lord, yes, but no one should go into battle unprepared. In fact, only a fool goes into battle without getting ready (Lk 14:31-32). Rather than rushing to war, we must learn to hold our horses until we are equipped.

Paul often refers to Christians as soldiers. One thing we learn from a good military is that it does not send new recruits immediately to the front lines. Instead, commanding officers take the time necessary to equip the soldiers so that they can become effective. The ancient Romans understood this principle. Consequently, even some of the most ferocious enemies were no match for the well-equipped Roman soldier. The Celts, for instance, were infamous for striking fear into their foes. According to one first-century BC historian, the Celts were terrifying. It wasn't just that they looked like wood-demons with shaggy hair, rippling muscles, and pasty white skin, but "with the armor which nature has given them, [*they*] *go naked into battle*."[4] It appears that before battle the Celtic warriors worked themselves into a frenzy. They painted their nude bodies; blew weird, discordant horns; chanted with harsh, deep voices; and beat their swords rhythmically against their shields to intimidate their enemies. (I, Joey, observed similar activities when I attended soccer matches in Scotland.) For much of their history, the Celtic strategy had worked well: that is, until Julius Caesar came to town in 55 BC.

Once Caesar encountered the Celts, he went back to Rome to prepare an army to face them. When Caesar returned a year later, he lined up his well-trained soldiers on the battlefield. True to form, the naked Celts sought to intimidate the Romans with their delirious pre-battle routine. Rather than fleeing in terror, as the Celts expected, the Roman soldiers marched fearlessly behind their commander toward the frenzied horde. The raucous notes and feverish enthusiasm of the Celts were no match for the armor and strength of Rome.

Today too many church leaders with genuine passion and contagious excitement show up to battle ill-equipped. While their enthusiasm can lead to some success, the spiritual forces and rulers of this dark world are not intimidated by Christian pompoms and face paint. Therefore, as soldiers of Christ, we must be trained in Scripture for teaching, correcting, and instructing believers in righteousness. Only when we can adequately handle

---

[4]Diodorus Siculus, *Library of History*, trans. C. H. Oldfather, LCL 340 (Cambridge, MA: Harvard University Press, 1939), 5.30.3 (p. 177).

the Word will we be able to fully help other believers be proficient and equipped for every good work (2 Tim 3:16-17). Such training, however, takes time, and it is foolhardy to rush into battle before one is ready.

> My students want to jump straight to application, asking how every point in a lecture applies to what they are doing in church next Sunday. My professor, Howard Hendricks, compared ministry to erecting a building; you need to lay a foundation first. He used to say, "Think of your theological education here like the construction of a huge building that you will use for your ministry. Today we are pouring concrete for the solid foundation. You, on the other hand, have shown up with a paintbrush."
>
> J. Daniel Hays, Old Testament scholar

Two young men in white shirts and ties show up at your door to discuss that the "Sabbath" has always been the seventh day. Why do Christians worship on Sunday? Rather than pontificate on why you think the Sabbath day was changed—an odd thought for folks who insist that Scripture remains the same—perhaps you should have spent some time studying the Jewish custom of the eighth day.

God began anew after resting on the seventh day (the original Sabbath). The eighth day then became a sign of new beginnings. The male child, the beginning of the next generation, was circumcised on which day? The eighth day. Luke describes the transfiguration as not six days later, as Mark does (Mk 9:2), but "about eight days" later (Lk 9:28). Was Luke fuzzy on the details? No. He wanted to emphasize the transfiguration as signaling something new, the new creation. When we hear the Gospels say "the first day of the week," we may be missing the reference to the eighth day. Christians don't worship on the Sabbath; we worship on the eighth day, the resurrection day, the day of new beginnings.

In case we failed to catch it in the Gospels, the author of the *Epistle of Barnabas* (written between AD 70 and AD 130) explains: "This is why we spend the eight day in celebration, the day on which Jesus both arose from the dead, and, after appearing again, ascended into heaven" (*Epistle of Barnabas* 15:8-9). We are not part of the old creation but the new.

So, why study before we rush into battle? Because biblical studies gives us a better answer for why Christians worship on Sunday. Studying will help you be prepared for the challenges of ministry.

EXEGESIS, EXEGESIS, AND YET MORE EXEGESIS

Donald Grey Barnhouse once said, "If I had only three years to serve the Lord, I would spend the first two in study." This quote so impressed Billy Graham that he commonly repeated it and urged it upon John Stott.[5] At first blush, this may seem like such an incredible notion that you're tempted to relegate it to hyperbole. But before you do, remember how long it took the Lord to get Moses ready for his ministry. It has been

---

[5]John Stott, *Your Mind Matters* (Downers Grove, IL: InterVarsity Press, 2006), 55.

quipped that Moses spent the first forty years of his life thinking he was a somebody, the next forty learning that he was a nobody, but the last forty discovering what God can do with a nobody.[6] Even more relevant, one should recall that Jesus did not launch his full-time ministry until he was around thirty years old. Furthermore, Jesus spent years giving his disciples biblical studies lessons before sending them out full time. And even then, the apostles put such a premium on prayer and ministry and study of the Word that they set themselves apart for it (Acts 6:3-4).

Rather than rushing into ministry, we must prepare ourselves to face the enemy, who delights in leading believers and unbelievers alike to misunderstand and misuse the Bible. In studying Scripture we seek proficiency in demolishing the arguments raised up against the knowledge of God. Through studying the Bible, we train to take captive every teaching and submit it to the truth of the gospel of Jesus Christ (2 Cor 10:4-6). Good exegesis must exist because bad exegesis must be answered. The great theologian Karl Barth understood this to be true so that when the Nazis were expelling him from Germany he offered these parting words to his students:

> We have been studying cheerfully and seriously. . . . And now the end has come. So listen to my last piece of advice: exegesis, exegesis and yet more exegesis! Keep to the Word, to the scripture that has been given us.[7]

---

[6]This is usually attributed to D. L. Moody.
[7]Eberhard Busch, *Karl Barth: His Life from Letters and Autobiographical Texts* (Philadelphia: Fortress Press, 1976), 531n236.

Fads Distract

My students were dismayed. Disappointment was plain on their faces. How could their beloved teacher not have read "the most important Christian book ever written"? I had just told them *Blue Like Jazz* had not yet made it on my reading list.[8] Now it's been fifteen years since the book was published and today (not to disparage the book) my students have never heard of it. Biblical studies is susceptible to fads like everything else. The church needs biblical scholars to help our congregations avoid fads that distract us from more important timeless truths. As C. S. Lewis writes:

> A man who has lived in many places is not likely to be deceived by the local errors of his native village; the scholar has lived in many times and is therefore in some degree immune from the great cataract of nonsense that pours from the press and the microphone of his own age.[9]

Study helps us discern between issues that are passing trends in our society and those of lasting significance for the kingdom of God. For instance, in Joey's generation Calvinism has made a comeback, led by theologians like John MacArthur, R. C. Sproul, J. I. Packer, Mark Dever, Mark Driscoll, and Voddie Baucham.[10] Of course, John Piper's writings and sermons have arguably had the most influence in this resurgence, raising an

---

[8]Donald Miller, *Blue Like Jazz* (Nashville: Thomas Nelson, 2002).

[9]C. S. Lewis, *The Weight of Glory and Other Addresses* (New York: Harper Collins, 2001), 58-59.

[10]See Collin Hansen's "Young, Restless, Reformed" in *Christianity Today* (September 2006), 32-38.

army of passionate young Calvinists, and even influencing rap music. Many Christian rap songs are now shot through with Reformed lyrics,[11] and some even include sound bites from Piper's sermons.[12] In fact, when I (Joey) was a college student, one passionate speaker nearly had me ready to ask John Calvin into my heart. I am embarrassed to say I started doing my quiet times from the Westminster Catechism. In comparison to Randy who describes himself as a "lousy Calvinist," today I like to tell people that I am a recovering Calvinist—on the mend from "Adult Onset Calvinism."[13]

To be sure, we both still have great respect for John Calvin. Joey recently finished reading Calvin's *Institutes*, and Randy intends to read them one day. But the extreme interest has all the hallmarks of a fad. It occurs to us that a danger of fads is that they determine (and thereby limit) the questions we ask and the scope of our study. In Randy's generation, the fad was eschatology. Much effort and energy was spent trying to prove or disprove that we were living in the last days. Avoiding the fads helps to keep our preparation broad. We need to spend the time and energy preparing well for the battles we will face tomorrow, which likely won't include today's fads.

---

[11]Matt Smethurst, "Where Did All These Calvinists Come From?" in *Christian Living* (October 2013), www.thegospelcoalition.org/article/where-did-all-these-calvinists-come-from.

[12]E.g., Tedashii (featuring Flame), "Make War" *Identity Crisis*, 2009.

[13]Stephen Altrogge, "Early Warning Signs of Adult Onset Calvinism," *The Blazing Center* (October 2015), http://theblazingcenter.com/2015/10/early-warning-signs-of-adult-onset-calvinism.html, accessed February 8, 2016.

Conclusion: Why do we need to learn *that*?

As Bible teachers we often hear students complain about what they are learning. "Why can't we just learn the practical stuff—the stuff that will help us in ministry?" The problem is, we don't know the future, so we don't know what you will need in the future.

As a part of a prison ministry, I am often amazed at the faith of my brothers behind bars. For instance, my first night there I found out that in order to attend worship services each week the inmates must endure a mandatory strip search. (Imagine my horror when I first misunderstood and thought they meant that I had to endure a strip search too.) Nevertheless, after the inmates put their clothes back on, they still entered the sanctuary with thanksgiving and praise. After my sermon that first night, I thought I would open up the floor for questions about the Bible. Since I am a tenured Bible scholar, I reckoned answering their questions would be as easy as a walk in the yard.

With unfounded confidence I called on the first inmate who raised his hand. He asked, "Dr. Dodson, why do we refer to Daniel by his Jewish name but to Shadrach, Meshach, and Abednego by their Babylonian names?" I responded with embarrassed "ums" and "uhs" as I admitted that I did not know. Figuring the questions couldn't get any harder, I then called on the second inmate. He said, "Psalm 88 is my favorite psalm. It begins by saying the psalm was written by Heman the Ezrahite. Who is Heman the Ezrahite?" I had no idea. The first inmate then said, "I have another question about names in the book of Daniel." To which I responded, "Oh look at the time! Sadly, I won't be able to answer any more questions." Learning about Babylonian naming practices might certainly seem like such a waste of time while you're sitting in a seminary classroom. "Why would we ever need to know about *that*?" would be a very understandable complaint. But, standing in a room full of prisoners, I wished I had learned a little something about it back when there was less at stake. Whether Babylonian names or some ancient adoptionist heresy, what you may consider pointless background material may be just what God has ordained for you to ready your horse for battle so that victory will belong to the Lord.

4

DON'T PLAY MARBLES
WITH DIAMONDS

■■■

WHEN I TEACH OUR FRESHMAN INTRODUCTION to ministry course, I often tell my students that we don't need any more mediocre ministers: "If you plan to be mediocre, go into some other field. Go into medicine, for instance. The worst thing a surgeon can do is kill someone. In ministry, you are messing with people's souls." "Oh, Dr. Richards," they exclaim with rolled eyes. Obviously, I am being humorous. But I'm not kidding. Biblical studies is serious business.

Christian songwriter Steve Camp once penned a stirring line about ministry. He accused Christians, saying, "We've been playing marbles with diamonds."[1] He meant that we were using sacred and powerful things, like prayer, worship, and the Word, for trivial purposes. While it works to use diamonds as marbles, what an incredible waste of diamonds it is. For example, we often use the "diamonds of Scripture" to play marbles when we draw transitory or even trite lessons from it. For example, rather than calling attention to its momentous role in salvation history, we

---

[1]Steve Camp, "Playing Marbles with Diamonds," *Justice Album* (1988).

use Jeremiah 29:11 as a slogan to embolden high school graduates.[2] Scripture becomes our spiritual ATM where we go to make a withdrawal whenever we are short of spiritual resources. Scripture does indeed have wonderful truths for beginning Christians, but there are also deep truths for those able to plumb the depths. If God has given you the blessings of a good mind, discipline, and the opportunity to study the Bible academically, don't play marbles with diamonds.

BAD EXEGESIS ABBREVIATES, DILUTES, OR EVEN DISTORTS THE GOSPEL

One way we play marbles with diamonds is in editing down the gospel. Like reading an abridged version of a book, my church tradition had abbreviated the gospel by stressing one aspect to the detriment of others. I grew up surrounded by passionate people preaching the good news that Christ came to reconcile humanity to God. "For it is by grace you have been saved, through faith" (Eph 2:8). This is absolutely true. Only later when studying the entire chapter of Ephesians 2 did I realize that there is more truth to be found in this chapter. Paul goes on to argue that God sought not only to reconcile people to himself through Jesus Christ but also to reconcile people *to each other*. Many Christians are aware that Paul was in prison when he wrote Ephesians, but they often don't know why. Paul had been accused (wrongfully) of taking a Gentile Christian into the Jews-only section of the temple (Acts 21). There was a wall dividing the two

---

[2]See E. Randolph Richards and Brandon O'Brien, *Misreading Scripture with Western Eyes* (Downers Grove, IL: InterVarsity Press, 2012), 192-96.

sections of the temple meant to keep the Gentiles out. According to Paul, Jesus demolished the dividing wall of hostility set up by ethnocentrism. Because of Christ's cross, despite one's cultural makeup, we are all one new people.[3]

This issue wasn't just dry theology for Paul. It was personal. He was in prison over an example of it. Believers are fellow citizens and equal parts of God's holy of holies (Eph 2:11-22). Because of the abbreviated gospel of my church, however, most of our invitations encouraged people to pray the sinner's prayer but not to repent of racism as well. Moreover, by emphasizing the individual aspect of salvation my church tradition had missed the community facet. But they diluted the individual aspect of it as well. Even for the individual, the radical, captivating, life-transforming story of Jesus Christ should impact every corner of our life. We are called to acknowledge Jesus as king. On the one hand, salvation costs us nothing, in the sense that we cannot purchase it for ourselves. We have nothing to offer to save our own souls. On the other hand, the gospel costs us everything. It is the treasure hidden in a field or the pearl of great price for which we must sell everything (Mt 13:44-46). My church had diluted the gospel down to four spiritual laws or even further to a three-point formula: Admit, Believe, and Confess. Dietrich Bonheoffer referred to this tendency as selling a gospel of cheap grace.[4]

---

[3]For more information about what Paul said about race, see E. Randolph Richards and Brandon O'Brien, *Paul Behaving Badly* (Downers Grove, IL: InterVarsity Press, 2016).

[4]Dietrich Bonhoeffer, *The Cost of Discipleship*, trans. R. H. Fuller (original German edition, 1937; repr., New York: Touchstone, 1995).

As a result, instead of learning the gospel as the kingdom of God breaking through on earth here and now, I was taught the Romans Road to salvation. Furthermore, rather than looking at Jesus' ministry to understand the gospel, our church watered the kingdom of God down to the promise of everlasting life in a heaven that's far, far away. Because of our stress on eternal destination, for us true religion was mostly "asking Jesus into my heart" rather than James's definition of forsaking worldliness and caring for orphans and widows (Jas 1:27).

I don't mean for these statements to come across as bitter or arrogant. I am deeply grateful for those people who invested what gospel they did know into my life, and I will consequently be forever indebted to them. These kind folks did the best they could and were faithful with what they had. They had not been fed by pastor-teachers trained in biblical studies. My church tradition tended to hire preachers to evangelize the occasional visitor more than pastor-teachers to equip faithful members.

> To put it bluntly, I grew up knowing exactly why Jesus died; I just didn't know why he lived. As Scot McKnight so admirably explained, we have reduced the gospel of Jesus Christ down to just personal salvation.[5] What was Jesus doing for three years? We wouldn't say it so crudely, but in my simplistic theology, he was just using time until the crucifixion. The Gospels, however, say that during those three years, Jesus was actually bringing the kingdom of God. My understanding of the Bible was too shallow.
>
> E. Randolph Richards, New Testament scholar

---

[5]Scot McKnight, *The King Jesus Gospel* (Grand Rapids: Zondervan, 2011).

BAD EXEGESIS HURTS PEOPLE

Not only does bad exegesis lead to an incomplete gospel, but it can also hurt people. In my first youth ministry, I was excited that a number of students from different cultural backgrounds began to attend. One night after a worship service, however, some church leaders ambushed me, saying that the black students weren't welcome. With righteous indignation and holy tears, I drove to the house of our chief elder, whose response paralyzed me: "You see, Joey, the Bible says that black people are *cursed*." He flipped his well-worn Bible to the story in Genesis where Noah gets drunk and curses Canaan. Completely mistaken but with genuine conviction, he argued that black people come from the cursed lineage of Canaan.[6] "That's why, you see, *we* can't worship with *them*." He had read his Bible a lot more than I had. I didn't even know the story. I regret to say that as a twenty-year-old kid who spent more time playing video games than reading the Old Testament, I didn't have the exegetical muscle to refute his historical and biblical fallacy. I felt in my heart that he was biblically wrong, but I didn't know enough to prove it. I had rushed in unprepared. The only thing I knew to do was resign. So we both lost. Those elders were wrong, but I was wrong too, because I had not studied. The answers were

---

[6]This gross misrepresentation of Scripture is often called the "Curse of Ham" (Canaan's father). Canaan is the one who is cursed. One of the other sons of Ham was Cush, who was associated with southern Egypt and thus Africa. Besides the fact that it was Canaan and not Cush who was cursed, to use the story to imply a curse upon all Africans is a dreadful misuse of Scripture and has been used historically to cause countless misery. For a fuller explanation and rebuttal, see J. Daniel Hays, *From Every People and Nation: a Biblical Theology of Race,* NSBT (Downers Grove, IL: InterVarsity Press, 2003); or Richards and O'Brien, *Paul Behaving Badly.*

there; I just didn't know them. Those young students also lost. They needed a biblically trained minister to defend them. Actually, the church lost, too. They needed a biblical scholar and they had hired me—they needed an owl but had hired a peacock.

Conclusion: But Good Exegesis . . .

Bad exegesis can hurt people and lead to dangerous conclusions, but we could tell you many wonderful stories about how good exegesis led to deeper understandings of the gospel and triumphant outcomes.

> In 1997 while at Wheaton College, New Testament scholar J. Julius Scott read to his New Testament Theology class this quote from C. H. Dodd:
>
> > "The ideal interpreter would be one who has entered into that strange first-century world, has felt its whole strangeness, has sojourned in it until he has lived himself into it, thinking and feeling as one of those to whom the Gospel first came; and who will then return into our world, and give to the truth he has discerned a body out of the stuff of our own thought."[7]
>
> This quote has left its mark on me since I first heard it and continues to be my passion and the chief aim in my scholarly vocation.
>
> Joel Willitts, New Testament scholar

---

[7]Charles Harold Dodd in his inaugural lecture on taking up the position of Norris-Hulse Professor of Divinity, delivered on Tuesday, June 2, 1936; reprinted as *The Present Task in New Testament Studies* (Cambridge: Cambridge University Press, 1936), 40-41.

My favorite story about the power of good exegesis comes from my son in the faith, L.J. Brooks. As a college freshman, L.J. bounded into my office to introduce himself. He spent more time, however, ogling my books than talking to me. Without asking my permission, he reached for my favorite Romans commentary and eagerly began fingering through it. I liked him immediately. My wife and kids did too, such that L.J. quickly became part of the family. For the next four years, he traveled with me as we preached to prisoners, college athletes, church members, and youth. Because he was a gifted speaker, a compassionate friend, and a talented athlete, L.J. soon became a popular and respected student on campus. During his senior year, L.J. applied and was accepted to Duke Divinity School. Everyone was proud and could not wait to see how God was going to use him in the future.

But the Lord surprised us all. One Friday afternoon L.J. called to tell me that he was in the hospital with an infection in his leg. "Dr. Dodson," he said, "they told me to prepare for the worst." L.J. died the next day. But rather than statements of bitterness or regret, his last words were "glory to God!"

As a father, I faced the challenge of navigating between my own grief and attempting to console my children who considered L.J. a Dodson. On hearing the news, my nine-year-old at the time groaned: "Why did God have to take L.J.? Why didn't God take a college student that we didn't like instead?" (I was afraid to ask him if he had a particular student in mind.) Rather, I told him about L.J.'s last words and how they related to a Greek exegetical paper L.J. had turned in to me earlier that week on 1 Thessalonians 4:13-14.

> Brothers and sisters, we do not want you to be uninformed about those who sleep in death, so that you do not grieve like the rest of mankind, who have no hope. For we believe that Jesus died and rose again, and so we believe that God will bring with Jesus those who have fallen asleep in him.

Later on that day I was writing the eulogy and picked up a book L.J. had borrowed from me. I quickly noticed a line that he had underscored and scrawled an exclamation point beside.

> Consume my life, my God, for it is Thine. *I seek not a long life but a full one*, like you, Lord Jesus.

It turns out the Lord had answered L.J.'s prayer, whose short-but-full life demonstrated for us how to live and how to die to the glory of God.

Sure, bad exegesis hurts people, but good exegesis changes lives . . . even in the face of death.

5

SPEAK THE LOCAL LANGUAGE

■ ■ ■

MY COLLEGE ROOMMATE BILLY married Irma from Monterrey, Mexico. She spoke English, but he didn't speak a word of Spanish when they started dating. He loved her deeply and plunged enthusiastically into language study. Every time I saw him he had a Spanish-English dictionary in his hand. "Why bother?" I asked. "Irma speaks English." He gently replied, "Randy, if I really want to hear her heart, I need to speak her heart language."

A passion to study God's Word should lead us to study the biblical languages (the Hebrew Old Testament and the Greek New Testament).[1] But while many students have enough passion to *start* learning the biblical languages, fewer have enough desire to stick with them. Sure, some students may lack the intellectual capacity to learn Hebrew and Greek, but most students fizzle because they lack motivation and discipline. They fail to acquire the biblical languages not because they cannot do so but because

---

[1] Parts of the Old Testament were written in Aramaic. For the sake of simplicity, however, we will focus on Hebrew and Greek.

they will not. Most scholars will tell you language learning involves delayed gratification. Some who quit language study excuse their lack of discipline by arguing that since we have so many great translations, learning Hebrew and Greek is superfluous. Ironically, a major reason for learning the biblical languages is raised in that argument. We learn the biblical language so that we can read the *Bible*—not a *translation* of the Bible. Reading a translation of the Bible is like kissing your spouse through saran wrap. Sure, you're making a connection, but it's just not the same.

Missionaries often say there is no substitute for speaking the local language. I (Randy) struggled to learn Indonesian. My wife cried a lot in language school—and I wanted to. We were motivated, though, by statements like "It gives you insight into the hearts of the people" or "You will never really understand a people until you speak their language." The hard work and tears paid off: those statements were true for us. So how is it that some Bible scholars are content to understand the Bible only through a translator? Reading a translation of the text is not the same as reading the text. It's the difference between watching your favorite film in standard definition rather than in high-def. Actually, it's worse than that. You're watching a foreign film and you're forced to rely on subtitles. To be sure, even with subtitles, you can still follow the dialogue and the plot. My wife and I first saw the movie *Driving Miss Daisy* while in Indonesia. We were the only two Americans in the theater. The movie was subtitled in Indonesian, so everyone followed the story, but we were the only two laughing. Miss Daisy, the elderly employer, told Hoke, her chauffeur, something witty. He replied, "Get out of here, Miss

Daisy!" We chuckled. Everyone else in the theater wondered why the employee was commanding his employer to get out of the car. They understood the words but missed the subtleties and nuances of the language *and culture*—a big part of the movie. Likewise, English-only readers of the Bible often fail to catch subtleties and nuances that are striking in the original languages.

> Greek will never be the tool you want it to be until you quit treating it like a tool and learn to love it for its own sake.
>
> Josh Richards, Classics scholar

SUBTLETIES AND NUANCES

We read Greek and Hebrew to catch the subtleties and nuances, such as the frequent word plays, in Scripture. We have word plays in English as well: "The other day a clown opened the door for me: it was a nice jester." A non-native speaker might miss the witticism in this sentence. When you have to point it out, it's not funny. God speaks to the prophet Jeremiah through puns. Puns are never funny once you translate them. Take the pun in Jeremiah 1 for instance:

> The word of the LORD came to me: "What do you see, Jeremiah?"
> "I see the branch of an almond tree [*shāqēd*]," I replied.
> The LORD said to me, "You have seen correctly, for I am watching [*shōqēd*] to see that my word is fulfilled." (Jer 1:11-12)

The translator can explain to you that almond tree (*shāqēd*) and watching (*shōqēd*) sound very similar. Now you see the pun, but admit it; it isn't funny anymore.

On a more serious note, the ancient biblical authors often connected passages together by repeating words, but translations can blur away those connections. What were supposed to be "Aha!" moments for us can be lost in translation. For example, the student reading Hebrew has a better chance of catching the parallel between God delivering Noah in an *ark* and Moses in a *basket*. In Hebrew, it's the same word, but translated differently. We were supposed to catch it and anticipate that God will deliver Moses from the waters just as he did Noah.

INTERPRETIVE OPTIONS

Those who learn biblical languages do so for more than just wordplays. They come to the text looking for interpretive *options*. They realize that there are often places in Scripture where the original languages raise a number of alternatives. Translators must decide on one for the reader. In the conversation between Jesus and Nicodemus in John 3, the Lord tells Nicodemus that in order to enter God's kingdom one must be born *anōthen*. This word can be translated "again" or "from above." Nicodemus takes *anōthen* as referring to being born again. Jesus plays on the other meaning of *anōthen* to stress how one must be born *from above*, from the Spirit of heaven. In fact, the Gospel of John loves to use words with multiple meanings, and expects the reader to catch all of them. Therefore, the Gospel likely intended the audience to catch both meanings in John 3. Unfortunately, an English translation can only use one of those meanings at a time. The other is lost. In a sense, as long as you're reading a translation, you are reading someone else's Bible— someone else's interpretation. Even if the translators chose the better interpretation, the English-only reader is likely unaware there were other options.

In other places, how a phrase is to be translated is actually debated. For example, in Luke 23:43, does Jesus say to the criminal on the cross beside him "I tell you, *today* you will be with me in paradise" or "I tell you *today*, you will be with me in paradise."[2] Would the thief be in paradise with Jesus that day (in a matter of hours), or did he find out that day that he would be with Jesus eventually (like at the Second Coming)? And how should we translate Galatians 2:16? Is a person justified "by faith in Christ" or "by the faithfulness of Christ?" Similarly, should the phrase in Habakkuk 2:4 be translated as "the righteous will live *by faith*" (as most English translations render it) or "*by faithfulness*" (as most Old Testament scholars think)?[3] Are the acts of edification, worship, thanksgiving, and submission listed in Ephesians 5:19-21 meant to detail the *results* of a Spirit-filled church or the *means* by which the church becomes Spirit-filled? This is not us musing. These are genuine options for translation that a translator decided for you, likely without you knowing.

What about Phoebe and Junia in Romans 16? Does Phoebe hold the office of *deaconess* in a Roman church or is she merely a *servant* to the churches? Likewise, is Junia a *prominent apostle*

---

[2]The original text did not have punctuation, so where we put the comma around *today* in this verse may have bearing on our understanding of the so-called intermediate state.

[3]Perhaps the English translators are interpreting Habakkuk 2:4 on the basis of their understanding of Romans 1:17 when they should be interpreting Romans 1:17 on the basis of the context of Habakkuk 2:4. See Michael F. Bird and Preston M. Sprinkle, eds., *The Faith of Jesus Christ* (Peabody, MA: Hendrickson, 2009).

or simply *well known to the apostles*? Should we take the women in 1 Timothy 3:11 as *women deacons,* or *wives of deacons*? Each of these is an option for translating the original phrase. Be careful. We shouldn't decide our theology and then translate the text to fit. Rather, we should study the Greek phrases, decide the accurate translation, and then allow it to shape our theology. So, was Phoebe a deaconess? Was the woman Junia an apostle? If you want to know, study Greek, research the passages, and decide for yourself. Stop allowing someone else to decide for you.

SUNDAY'S COMING

> We do Greek on Monday because we have to preach next Sunday.
>
> Preben Vang, New Testament scholar

James warns us that preachers and teachers will be judged more strictly than others (Jas 3:1). Youth ministers often use James's warning about tongues starting fires to caution youth against gossiping, but James was warning teachers. If the love of Christ does not drive us to study the biblical languages, then the fear of God should. We study Hebrew and Greek so that we can be better teachers and preachers. We've heard many preachers toss Hebrew and Greek words and their "definitions" from the pulpits. Although using Hebrew and Greek to decorate a sermon is usually harmless, it can mislead the congregation to believe that a particular Hebrew or Greek word has a clear English meaning. But in truth, it's the context of a sentence that shapes the meaning of a word. Let's use an English example. What does *pretty* mean?

"Attractive," we might reply. Well, that's a *pretty* good definition. As you see, the meaning for *pretty* depends on its context. *Trunk* can mean several things, depending on whether the context is an elephant, a description of luggage, or a rack of swimming garments. Likewise, ḥesed does not mean "lovingkindness," it means ḥesed and can be translated in a number of ways in English. In fact, we do not have an English word that comes close enough to capturing its meaning. In some contexts *pneuma* translates as human spirit and in some it translates as the divine Spirit (and sometimes it just means wind). Who will teach the next generation of God's people these subtleties and nuances? Who will help unravel confusing translations? Who will help them understand the roles of Phoebe and Junia? If not you, who?

> And that was it. Like tee-totaling Liza Hamilton in John Steinbeck's *East of Eden*, who is never again entirely sober after her doctor orders a sip of whiskey at bedtime. I never walked away. I was and I remain intoxicated by the Greek New Testament.[4]
>
> Beverly Roberts Gaventa, New Testament scholar

CONCLUSION

For Bible scholars the biblical languages are the cornerstone. New insights from both secular and biblical Greek studies are opening up fresh ways of reading the New Testament. Hebrew, Aramaic, and Greek writings from the intertestamental period

---

[4]Beverly Roberts Gaventa, "A Word of Gratitude" in *I (Still) Believe: Leading Bible Scholars Share Their Stories of Faith and Scholarship*, eds. John Byron and Joel Lohr (Grand Rapids: Zondervan, 2015), 84.

are still largely understudied. What discoveries are waiting? There is so much unexplored territory for young scholars to search and survey.[5] But this requires one to read the languages. Sometimes ministers will say that it is not necessary to learn Hebrew and Greek. Bill Mounce tells first year Greek students, "The only people I have heard say that Greek is not important are those who do not themselves know Greek. Strange."[6] While many ministers don't read Hebrew and Greek well, *every* Bible scholar must if they are going to handle the Word of God correctly.

Will you step up to the challenge?

---

[5]For more on new advancements in secular Greek studies and the ramifications for biblical Greek, see Constantine R. Campbell, *Advances in the Study of Greek* (Grand Rapids: Zondervan, 2015). See also Steven E. Runge and Christopher J. Fresch, *The Greek Verb Revisited* (Bellingham, WA: Lexham Press, 2015); and Timothy Michael Law, *When God Spoke Greek* (Oxford: Oxford University Press, 2013). For the latest on Hebrew studies, see the Eisenbrauns series Linguistic Studies in Ancient West Semitic—LSAWS, www.eisenbrauns.com/ECOM/_4PC10P3RG.HTM.
[6]William D. Mounce, *Basics of Biblical Greek*, 3rd edition (Grand Rapids: Zondervan, 2009), 4.

KEEP THE MAIN THING
THE MAIN THING

■ ■ ■

STUDYING SCRIPTURE IS MESMERIZING AND FUN.
Uncovering hidden treasures, both old and new (Mt 13:52), can
be intoxicating, even seductive. One common danger in biblical
studies, however, is that we can feed the head and neglect the
heart so that there is a temptation to prize knowledge of God
more than knowing God. Bible scholars can be somewhat like
the hunter in one of Aesop's fables who asked the woodsman if
he'd seen any lion tracks. Familiar with the area, the woodsman
knew exactly where the lion was. He said to the hunter, "If you're
looking for the lion, I can take you directly to him." At this, the
hunter trembled and said, "No, I wasn't trying to find the lion, I
was looking only for his tracks!"

As ludicrous as that may seem, Bible scholars can get so fixed
on the fascinating prints of God in his Word that they fail to
follow the trail to the end, to him. We must not be like the
Pharisees who studied the Scriptures diligently but still failed
to respond to the truth they pointed to (Jn 5:39). As Richard
Bauckham warns young scholars, a great peril of studying the
Bible academically is that "it can seem that the more carefully

one understands how a text spoke to its original historical context the less it speaks to us."[1]

Don't Dry Up

In a lecture on the peril of theological education draining the soul, John Coe stated, "Despite many of [education's] wonders, it surreptitiously and ever so slowly distanced me from myself, God and others. The language of education drowned out the language of prayer, for the latter was not a necessary tool in my becoming proficient in the academy." This is a danger for everyone engaged in deep academic study of the Word. As knowledge increases, one's spirit can wither simultaneously. Knowing how to pray, how to

> Every semester I tell my students this line attributed to Justin Joffer: "Many books in the world can convey truth to us, but only one reveals God. If we use the Bible only to pursue truths rather than to pursue God, it becomes just another book on the bestsellers list."
>
> John Walton, Old Testament scholar

wait, how to be silent, or how to listen to God is not required to make the grade, and busy students often cut back to just what is required. But while this is a common danger, it is *not* an inevitable fate. Many students find their souls enriched by the academic

---

[1]Richard Bauckham, "A Life with the Bible" in *I (Still) Believe: Leading Bible Scholars Share Their Stories of Faith and Scholarship*, ed. John Byron and Joel N. Lohr (Grand Rapids: Zondervan, 2015), 28.

study of the Word. This enrichment doesn't happen accidently or automatically. You'll drift if you don't make an effort. It's not that academic study causes a dry spiritual life; rather, neglecting our spiritual life causes us to dry up, even if what we are studying is God's Holy Word. Someone who refuses to eat will starve to death even if they are working in a pastry shop.

Too Busy Not to Pray

How do we avoid this pitfall? By humbly praying for the Lord to help us totally apply ourselves to his Word and then totally apply his Word to ourselves.[2] Ben Sira, a scholar of the Law and the Prophets who lived about two centuries before Jesus was born, listed prayer as essential for a scholar of the Word: "He sets his heart to rise early to seek the Lord. . . . He opens his mouth in prayer" (Sir 39:5, NRSV). Although it seems intuitive that as Bible scholars we would humble ourselves before the Lord and ask his Spirit to guide us before we study his Word, it becomes so easy—due to the pressures of time and busy schedules—to let prayer fall to the wayside. As A. G. Sertillanges put it, "Study must first of all leave room for worship, prayer, [and] direct meditation on the things of God."[3] Can students of the Bible become too busy to pray? Alas, it happens, and often under the guise of piety.

It was the day of my seminary Hebrew final. I (Joey) rolled out of bed at 4 a.m. to throw down a Red Bull and a Pop-Tart

---

[2]This comes from a Latin motto that appeared on the opening pages of the Nestle Greek New Testament for many years: *Te totum applica ad textum; rem totam applica ad te* (Apply yourself totally to the text; apply the text totally to yourself).

[3]A. G. Sertillanges, *The Intellectual Life*, trans. Mary Ryan, 3rd ed. (Washington, DC: The Catholic University of America Press, 1998), 28.

(the breakfast of champions) so that I could cram some Semitic syntax into my head a few hours before the exam. I had recently recommitted to praying through one Psalm before I started each day. That morning I felt a holy tug on my heart to pray through the day's passage, Psalm 34, before I began to study. But I had a Hebrew final! Since I was learning God's Old Testament language, surely he wouldn't mind me skipping my prayer time. Besides, I thought, maybe I could hit Psalm 34 after the exam. And with that justification, I gave it no further thought and began to study. I walked into the classroom at 8 a.m. and sat down as the professor was passing out the test. He said, "The final exam has only one passage for you to translate, a Psalm of David." Do you see where this is going? Sure enough, I turned over the page to see the words "Translate Psalm 34." I think I heard God laughing. As I struggled for hours through the unfamiliar Psalm, I couldn't help but to chuckle too. Indeed, God has a good sense of humor.

Don't misunderstand me here. I'm not saying that I should have read my devotional so that I would have done better on the exam. Rather, God used an ironic moment to remind me that I had become so engrossed in the menu that I was forgetting to order. I was crowding out my spiritual life with academic study. When we study to the point that we give up prayer, we are playing a fool's game.[4]

This is not a twenty-first-century problem. Nor do we need a twenty-first-century solution. We are not the first to find ourselves busy. Two thousand years ago, Cicero noted that busyness

---

[4]Ibid., 29.

was the lazy man's excuse for not doing what needs to be done.[5] Martin Luther holds a premier place in church history—in addition to being the father of the Protestant Reformation, he was

> Here's a quote from Helmut Thielicke's *A Little Exercise for Young Theologians* that still speaks to me today:
>
> > Now it is almost a devilish thing that even in the case of the theologian the joy of possession can kill love. . . . So the theologian, and not least the young theologian, gets into a horrible internal conflict. . . . In his reflective detachment the theologian feels himself superior to those who, in their personal relationship to Christ, completely pass over the problems of the historical Jesus or demythologizing or the objectivity of salvation. This disdain is a real *spiritual disease*. This conflict is precisely *the* disease of theologians.
>
> Benjamin Reynolds, New Testament scholar

a professor, pastor, and author. It's fair to say he was a busy, busy man. On one occasion, he was asked about his plans for the next week. He noted that he customarily spent two hours a day in prayer. However, the coming week was going to be extra busy: "Work, work from early till late. In fact, I have so much to do that I shall spend the first *three hours* in prayer."[6] Likewise, for the beginning Bible scholar, there is so much to learn, read, and

---

[5]Cicero, *Letters to Atticus* 5.11.
[6]Martin Luther as quoted in J. O. Sanders, *Spiritual Leadership* (Chicago: Moody, 1974), 76.

write. You need plenty of time in prayer to help us accomplish this. What you will find is that "our study informs our prayers, and our prayers enliven our study."[7] And if you don't take care of the important, the urgent will rule your life.

DON'T BE A HERMIT

Biblical scholarship is not an individual pursuit. It's a corporate endeavor. But because of our focus and passion, Bible scholars can easily become hermits. God gave us all of Scripture and created us for community. Like living stones, we need to come together to edify one other and to build an academy whose scholarship is acceptable to God.

At Tyndale House, University of Cambridge, Bible scholars have almost every book they could want on a shelf right in front of them. There are desks scattered among the shelves. It is Shangri-La for a Bible scholar. I have worked there for hours without noticing a minute passing, only to realize my neck was cramped and my bum was numb. It was a happy misery. But twice a day, a gong is struck and *all* scholars are expected to stop what they're doing and convene in the break room for tea. No excuses accepted. "But I'm right in the middle of something critical," whined in the most scholarly and self-important tone, is not accepted. The gong is always an interruption. Nonetheless, most scholars will look back and say those break times were the best times. Fellowship, camaraderie, important dialogue, and exchange of ideas occurred. Friendships were forged. Some of my best academic insights occurred during those "interruptions."

---

[7]Kelly M. Kapic, *A Little Book for New Theologians* (Downers Grove, IL: InterVarsity Press, 2012), 70.

CONCLUSION: DON'T MAJOR ON THE MINOR

An important part of keeping the main thing the main thing is not being sidetracked into minor things. It's not only important to read widely with respect to books of the Bible but also to interact with a wide range of scholars—not just evangelical scholars. It's easier to criticize someone you don't know—to brush aside their work because of where they went to school, what church tradition they represent, or even who their friends are. And let's face it: a judgmental attitude is often our default setting. But the pursuit of biblical studies is best done in a diverse community, that is, diverse with regard to age, tradition, culture, denomination, and so on.

Encountering Bible teachers in other cultures caused me to read and study the Bible differently. I was raised in a Baptist church that considered drinking alcohol an almost "unpardonable" sin. You can imagine my shock at a conference in Barcelona, Spain. After my first lecture, Jens, the college pastor of a group of undergraduates from a Brethren congregation in Germany said, "Hey Joey, our church bought some beer if you want to come." I sputtered, "You guys *drink* at your church?" He responded: "Of course we do. We're Christians, not Muslims." Whereas I associated teetotalism with genuine Christianity, my German friend associated it with Islam. Don't miss the point by getting into an argument for or against Christians drinking alcohol in moderation. My Bible tradition had turned teetotalism into one of the fundamental doctrines of the faith. We had turned a minor into a major.

While serving in Indonesia, I really made a misstep. Christians there consider playing pool (billiards) to be serious sin.

"What?" I exclaimed. "We had a pool table in my house growing up." I thought I had set the record straight. Years later I learned that the church regularly thanked God for saving me from the sinkhole of sin where I had been raised. My dad the deacon would have been appalled. They had turned a minor into a major.

When I was living in Germany, a fellow Christian scholar invited me to come over to watch a movie with his small group. When I agreed, he added a heads up, "Now, Joey, it's rated R, but don't worry. It's for nudity not violence." I was taken aback. In my American circles, we were just the opposite. We were more okay with a film showing people pulverized by bombs and bullets as long as everyone kept their clothes on. Again, don't get lost arguing over whether or not one should watch violent movies with or without nudity. Rather, note that traveling to these cultures helped us see blind spots in our own perspectives. I never considered whether Christians should be concerned about watching violent movies. By studying with those who were different than us, we realized that what we thought were major issues were really minor and vice versa.

We weren't the first "Bible scholars" to focus on the minor and miss the major. Jesus complained about the Bible scholars of his day focusing on the minor and missing the major. While most of us are familiar with Jesus' conflicts with the Pharisees in the Gospels, we may never have noticed that the theme of justice from the Old Testament prophets stands behind many of his rebukes.[8] The religious leaders in Jesus' day were concerned with

---

[8]See J. Daniel Hays, "'Sell Everything You Have and Give to the Poor': The Old Testament Prophetic Theme of Justice as the Connecting Motif of Luke 18:1–19:10." *JETS* 55/1 (2012), 43-63.

doing the law—what God wanted—but they had forgotten what the *prophets* had said God wanted. For instance, Micah writes:

> And what does the LORD require of you?
> To act justly and to love mercy
> and to walk humbly with your God. (Mic 6:8)

In Luke's Gospel, Jesus constantly adjures the Pharisees to live according to the spirit of the law, and not just the letter. For instance, once while Jesus is dining with some of these religious leaders, he lashes out at them:

> Woe to you Pharisees, because you give God a tenth of your mint, rue and all other kinds of garden herbs, but you neglect justice and the love of God. You should have practiced the latter without leaving the former undone. Woe to you Pharisees, because you love the most important seats in the synagogues and respectful greetings in the marketplaces. (Lk 11:42-43)

In short, the religious leaders had forgotten to act justly, to love mercy, to walk humbly.

Later in Luke, Jesus is again dining with some Pharisees. In response to their petty maneuvering to sit at the VIP table, Jesus launches into a stern lecture on what it looks like to walk humbly before the Lord:

> When someone invites you to a wedding feast, do not take the place of honor. . . . For all those who exalt themselves will be humbled, and those who humble themselves will be exalted. (Lk 14:8, 11)

Likewise, in Luke 18 Jesus tells a parable about a self-righteous Pharisee and a self-effacing tax collector. Whereas the pompous Pharisee trumpeted before everyone at the temple about his piety, which involved no justice or mercy, the crestfallen tax collector stood from afar, bowed his head, beat his chest and bawled: "God, have mercy on me, a sinner."

Luke brings this series of Jesus' confrontations with the Pharisees to a head with the story of a real tax collector, Zacchaeus, in chapter 19. Zacchaeus is the living embodiment of Jesus' earlier parable of the tax collector—the one who pleaded with God to have mercy on him. But more subtly than that, Zacchaeus also does all that Micah enjoined. He acts justly ("If I have cheated anybody . . . I will pay back"), he loves mercy ("I will give half of my possessions to the poor"), and he humbly climbs the sycamore tree. Because of his actions, Jesus pronounces that salvation has come to his house.

The Pharisees paid careful attention to the commands to tithe, to avoid unclean things, and to adhere to the Sabbath. Yet, they neglected the "weightier matters." They had not kept the main thing the main thing. The Pharisee in the temple noted how he was doing better than the tax collector in so many ways, yet he himself had failed in the most important ways. As you delve into biblical studies, filling your head with all kinds of wonderful knowledge, don't neglect your heart and your hands.

DON'T GET PUFFED UP

■ ■ ■

ALTHOUGH ALL PEOPLE ARE prone to pride, training in biblical scholarship can aggravate our hubris all the more. We are taught to look critically at other scholars' methodologies, arguments, and conclusions, and we can become professional cynics, doubting everything and questioning everyone. Although there is a role for these things in scholarship, we should do them in meekness and with kindness. Our conceit, however, can hinder us from being gracious to one another.

> Studying Bible and theology can be a life-changing invasion into a person's innermost self. That change, however, can create pretentiousness. Mastery of the thought of Moses or Isaiah or Jesus or Paul . . . can become third-person theology. That is, the young theologian can begin to identify so much with the thoughts of one of these greats that he or she begins to think that theologian's thoughts are his or her own. . . . Until the young theologian has studied long enough to know what he or she has actually acquired personally, we should hearken to the great words of the German theologian Helmut Thielicke and not pretend to a theology that is not yet ours.[1]
>
> Scot McKnight, New Testament scholar

---

[1]Helmut Thielicke, *A Little Exercise for Young Theologians* (Grand Rapids: Eerdmans, 1962), loc. 172.

Our pride shows itself when we begin to compare ourselves with others.[2] When we do so, we become either jealous because someone has outdone us, or smug as we look upon those we have outstripped. When I was in seventh grade I encountered a man who was 6'9". Since I was a vertically challenged basketball player, I was always jealous of tall people. I approached the giant and asked, "Sir, do you play basketball?" In response, he looked down at me and scowled. "No, kid. Do you play miniature golf?" This insecurity I felt as a short basketball player carried over to my career as a Bible scholar. I struggled with comparing myself to others whom I felt towered over me. I have to remind myself that my competency has always been and will always be from the Lord.

Comparing ourselves to others has a ditch to avoid on the other side of the road. That is, we can exalt ourselves at the expense of others. It seems in Paul's day there were some Christians who looked down on Paul, saying he had gotten his gospel secondhand. They had followed Jesus during his earthly ministry but Paul was a Johnny-come-lately (Gal 1). Others viewed themselves as "super apostles," considering themselves far better skilled than Paul in public speaking (2 Cor 11:5-6). They bragged to the Corinthians that they were professional ministers (paid to do ministry) while Paul was only bivocational (2 Cor 11:7-9). Like them, we can become so self-absorbed in our accomplishments manifested in our degrees, positions, and publications that we look down on others whom God cherishes.

For example, I was attending a professional meeting and was perusing through some new books that were freshly published.

---

[2]The comparison game is an ancient problem. See Plato, *Apology* 20d-21d.

A publisher-friend walked up and said, "Randy, do you know the first thing many scholars do when they pick up a book?" I shook my head no. He replied, "They look in the index to see if they were quoted." I sheepishly realized I had done just that. When conceit comes, I am reminded of what the Lord said to Baruch, Jeremiah's scribe. Baruch's world was at the brink of disaster, but

> One of the things that I have realized (slowly) is that my route to becoming, or my way of being, a biblical scholar is unlike anyone else's. Each of us has a path and a set of skills that allows us to operate faithfully in our calling. But if you find the balance between joy and labor as a biblical scholar, then you'll be a great success.
>
> Madison Pierce, New Testament scholar

the scribe was more concerned with himself than he was with the Lord's people. Therefore, God said to Baruch: "Should you then seek great things for yourself? Do not seek them" (Jer 45:5). Similarly, my selfish ambition often gets the best of me so that I am more concerned with my popularity as a Bible scholar than I am with employing my knowledge of the Bible to comfort those whose world has been overturned.

Paul told the Philippians:

Brothers and sisters, I do not consider myself yet to have taken hold of it. But one thing I do: Forgetting what is behind and straining toward what is ahead, I press on toward the goal to win the prize for which God has called me heavenward in Christ Jesus. (Phil 3:13-14)

Paul was talking about the ultimate goal of the heavenward call of God in Christ Jesus, but in context—remember that context matters—Paul had been talking about making the necessary sacrifices for the ministry that God had given him (to be the apostle to the Gentiles).

But whatever were gains to me I now consider loss for the sake of Christ. What is more, I consider everything a loss because of the surpassing worth of knowing Christ Jesus my Lord, for whose sake I have lost all things. I consider them garbage (*skybala*), that I may gain Christ. (Phil 3:7-8)

Thus, Paul's word is timely here also. Paul considered his advanced theological training to be *skybala* (dung) when compared to knowing Christ. Yet, his advanced training wasn't actually

During my student days, I approached a major scholar whose methodology I had adopted and asked if he would read a paper I had written. I was shocked when he replied, "I would be honored to learn from your work!" His words struck me and have stuck with me. His stature didn't make him complacent or arrogant. I resolved in that moment to always consider myself a student. I tell my classes that I'm the "lead student" and that they're responsible to participate in my learning. That preserves me from arrogance and encourages them to freely and vigorously participate. It's just a small way to embody humility as a scholar.

Timothy Gombis, New Testament scholar

skybala. Context! He had just bragged about it (Phil 3:4-6). It was *skybala* only when compared to the unbelievable value of knowing Christ. Even as valuable as his training was—how incredibly useful it had proven to be for the kingdom—it was dung when compared to knowing Christ.

Your training in biblical studies will be valuable. Don't ever consider it rubbish (except when comparing it to knowing Christ). Don't ever demean another person's training. The context of Paul's *skybala* remark shows that it was a given that his advanced training and pedigree were a true treasure. Paul stresses (by hyperbole) that diamonds are just gravel when compared to the unsurpassed treasure of knowing Christ.

> As biblical scholars we are often encouraged to be critical. As a woman biblical scholar, I was sometimes encouraged to be hard and tough. The academic world can be surprisingly lacking in kindness, encouragement, and prayer. Studying Scripture should always push us to love more deeply, reflect more richly. This is true as teachers and as scholars. I seek opportunities to build friendships rather than to "network." It leads to deep and abiding academic friendships for this life journey.
>
> Beth M. Stovell, Old Testament scholar

We realize that pride comes before a fall, even for Bible scholars (or, should I say, especially for Bible scholars). How do we deal with this pride? According to John Calvin there's no other remedy to pride than to rid ourselves of the two most noxious pests: self-love and vain-glory.[3] Of course, we are impotent to do so without the grace of God and the power of his Holy Spirit. Therefore, each morning I pray the Lord will help me not to be prideful. When I fail, God answers my prayers by using my friends and family to keep me humble. For example, I like to tour archaeological sites like ancient Corinth, Sardis, or Laodicea. I bring back hundreds of pictures. My wife sighs and says, "Randy, it's a picture of a pile of rocks." Well, yes, it is a pile of rocks, but I have pictures of that pile of rocks from the north side and another viewed from the south. I can look at my pictures for hours, imagining what things would have looked like when they weren't piles of rocks. I could stand in the hot Turkish sun for an hour just running my hands over a fallen column, imagining that Paul might have placed his hand there. "Paul walked through this very gate into the city. My, oh my." But I cannot expect everyone to love the details I love. After all, my wife is correct. It *is* a pile of rocks. Thank God for using our faithful friends and family—if we will listen to them—to remind us that the condition of our heart is more impressive than the prestige of our degree or what I discovered on an archeological dig.

Earlier chapters encouraged you not to be lazy or brash, to follow your passions, and to study deeply. While the Ephesian church worked hard and had patient endurance, tested what they heard and rooted out heresy, Jesus had this against them: they forgot their first love (Rev 2:1-4). It's possible God has gifted you with more talent than average. If you are faithful as a Bible

---

[3]John Calvin, *The Institutes of Christian Religion*, 3.7.4.

scholar, God may even increase the talents within you (Mt 25:29). Humility may not *yet* be a challenge for you. Your skills are perhaps still meager. Invitations to serve may be modest and few. But if you work hard in biblical studies, and are faithful in the little things, he may later entrust great things to you (Lk 19:17). Pray now that should such a day come, God will give you family, mentors, and friends to keep you humble.

8

BIBLICAL STUDIES
IS AN EQUAL
OPPORTUNITY VOCATION

■ ■ ■

THIS CHAPTER IS WRITTEN FOR OUR black, Hispanic, Asian, and female readers—Bible scholars whose voices are so needed in our field. Yes, we are very aware of the irony of two white guys writing about the role of women, black, brown, Hispanic, or Asian scholars, the marginalized, and those in the emerging world in biblical studies. But the topic is too important to skip. For this reason, we enlisted help from some colleagues to construct five challenges.

STEP UP TO THE PLATE

We encourage female, black, Hispanic, and non-Western scholars to step up and do the hard work of biblical studies. We are *not* suggesting that somehow you haven't or that somehow you must do more than the others. Jarvis J. Williams is an African American New Testament scholar who has written four major monographs and numerous scholarly articles on Pauline soteriology in its Second Temple Jewish context. As an established scholar, he offers this exhortation:

I regularly pray that God would raise up many, many more black and brown New Testament scholars. But before this will happen, black and brown men and women intellectually gifted and motivated to give themselves to a life of biblical scholarship must stop believing the lie that just because they are black or brown, they should necessarily pursue practical ministry training instead of rigorous academic training. And they must avoid earning the kind of master's and doctoral degrees that have no academic value in the guild of New Testament studies. Instead, they must go hard after pursuing a rigorous graduate degree grounded in biblical studies and ancient languages and a PhD from a legitimate program that will enable them to acquire the most technical and necessary skills to devote themselves to a lifetime of critical NT scholarship. The field is ripe for more black and brown NT scholars, but it will not welcome them unless they are properly trained![1]

We want to join Dr. Williams in encouraging new black and brown (and female) biblical scholars to rise to the challenge. Perhaps a good way for us to do this is by citing a few examples

---

[1]Jarvis prefers the terms *black* and *brown*. Another friend prefers *African American*. In South Florida, my Cuban, Puerto Rican, Columbian, and Argentinean friends do not self-designate as "brown." Generally, they accept Hispanic or Latino, terms the mainstream media seem to consider interchangeable. They tell me Hispanic tends to focus on Spanish-speaking origin, while Latino tends to be more geographic (Latin American origin). They prefer to be called Puerto Rican or Columbian or Chilean, etc. For the sake of space, I hope my friends will be gracious and forgiving if I just use "black" and "Hispanic." Similarly, we hesitate to use some lump term like "minority scholars" to summarize the list, because women are likely the majority in the world and the sum of the others is likely more than the so-called majority. Labels never work. Jesus will call us each by name.

of those who have done so. Bernie Cueto is an accomplished New Testament scholar. He is a Cuban scholar who earned his position the same hard way that everyone else did. There was no shortcut for Dr. Cueto.

In addition to being a strong Bible teacher, Dr. Cueto is a gifted preacher. I often tease that he could preach squirrels down out of trees. He's the best preacher I know. He grounds his sermons in solid biblical exegesis and then delivers them with practiced eloquence. He shares:

> Growing up as a Hispanic in a city that was the epitome of diversity afforded me an incredible cultural education. Unbeknownst to me, this cultural education would greatly impact my theological formation. Miami in the 80s and 90s included different voices (perspectives) with different rhythms and balance.
>
> We needed each other to see the complete picture. I had Brazilian friends who would play soccer with the speed of a track star and balance of a prima ballerina, all while talking to me in Portuguese. As an American of Cuban descent the only thing I knew about a ball was that it was to be thrown at a bat as hard as possible. I had friends from Jamaica who would teach me their native Patois in unique rhythms.
>
> Although I always appreciated the melting pot of my hometown, I did not fully value its impact on my life until I started pursuing biblical studies as a vocation in another state. It has been almost two decades since then. The diversity in the academy is not what it can be, but it certainly has come a long way. Appreciation for precision, depth, and clarity in solid biblical scholarship is now coupled with an enhanced desire for differing cultural voices (perspectives), scholars with various speeds and balance, and rhythms. The young scholar, instead of obsessing

over, "Can I make it?" or "Can I fit in?" should look at the opportunity of coming from a different background and say, "I can
contribute to this ancient and heavenly conversation in a way
that others might not be able to see just yet. I see something they
might be missing." Evangelicalism not only needs the Hispanic
or Latino scholar to notice what might be missed, but they can
shine the light on something that must not be missed. The life of
the mind will mold your character on the anvil of scholarship. It
will give you a unique opportunity to contribute to the field of
biblical studies in a way that will challenge our thinking and
sharpen how we think about God, the text, and his culturally
diverse world.

Lynn Cohick represents another example of one who has paid
the price of diligence, commitment, and sacrifice to become an
exceptional Bible scholar. It's possible her gender helps her
notice some insights, just as her experience on the mission field
no doubt has also helped her, but the bulk of her insights came
from her hard work in the trenches of New Testament scholarship. Dr. Cohick noted:

Paul traveled around the Eastern Roman Empire teaching the
gospel, and Priscilla likewise lived in three major cities (Corinth,
Ephesus and Rome), teaching and instructing disciples. Why is
it so hard for female scholars, for me, to live into this? Here is
where encouragement becomes so important. Years ago a colleague said to me, after reading an admittedly poor chapter draft,
"I don't see Lynn in this work." He encouraged me to push myself
and realize potential. More recently, another colleague advised
me, "You have been asked to speak at this gathering. You have
something to say. Say it." I needed to hear that I was not the

"token" woman, but could use that platform to speak what I believed needed to be said. Both these male colleagues gave me a gift—of being myself, a scholar who as a woman brings a fullness to scholarship for the church.

Another great example is Kathy whom I (Randy) call one of the "young guns" on my faculty. Although I serve at a very conservative evangelical university, she is chair of our Department of Biblical Studies. I asked her to share a few thoughts for this chapter:

> While there were few women in my graduate programs, the landscape is changing. Female scholars are enjoying new opportunities in evangelical academia. Usually. There will likely continue to be pockets within the evangelical academy that are not receptive to female voices. In response, collaboratively work for change from the inside. Know yourself, your abilities, and your context.

DON'T LET OTHERS LABEL OR LIMIT YOU

Bernie's contribution is not *necessarily* a Cuban reading of the New Testament. The major contribution of the Latino biblical scholar is not, first and foremost, to be a *Latino* scholar, but to be an excellent scholar who is also Latino. Bernie's heritage no doubt helps him to see things in the text that I would overlook, but he cannot and should not be pigeonholed.

Dr. Joubert Sumanti is an Indonesian scholar in New Testament studies. I would never suggest that all an Indonesian scholar can do is an "Indonesian reading" of, for example, John 9. It's wrong to imply such a scholar could not present an insightful reading of John 9 that is independent of his cultural heritage. On the other hand, an Indonesian reading will likely provide fresh insights. Thus, we must resist limiting black, brown, Hispanic, Asian, or woman scholars to areas with that imprimatur, while simultaneously recognizing that their heritage or gender can and should bring perspective that my white male viewpoint cannot or does not see. Don't allow the church or the academy to limit you.

Don't Label or Limit Yourself

Just as we insist that others not label or limit you, we challenge you not to label or limit yourself. Years ago, when I was teaching in rural northern Arkansas, I had an especially gifted student named Carla. It was no surprise to me to hear that she was accepted into Yale Divinity School. Not long after, however, I received a message from her: "Dr. Richards, Nick and I are expecting!" The good news seemed to her so untimely. How could she move across the country and start a graduate program with a newborn? What's more, for her church tradition, she was already pushing boundaries with an advanced degree in theology. What business did she have pursuing a doctorate? What would she do with it? Should she even go? One of my proudest moments was when I encouraged her not to limit herself but to go seize the day. Eventually earning a PhD from Princeton, Carla became an accomplished New Testament scholar and now teaches at a seminary.[2] She and Nick (a pastor) are wonderful parents to two fine children.

The experience isn't unique to Randy's student Carla. Similarly, my wife, Sadie Dodson, considered dropping out of her

---

[2]See, e.g., Carla S. Works, *The Church in the Wilderness*, WUNT 2/379 (Tübingen: Mohr Siebeck, 2014).

master's program when she found out that she was pregnant with our firstborn child. Nevertheless, to be faithful in fulfilling her calling, she stuck with it and stayed in her classes—jammed into classroom desks not designed for the pregnant. I was amazed that not only did my wife navigate through morning sickness, a caesarean section, and nursing as a full-time student, but she graduated with a perfect grade point average. Our daughter, Mattie Mae, wants to be a professor. Of course she does. She was listening to lectures in the womb.

Our universities draw students from a wide range of church traditions. Some traditions encourage women in ministry; other traditions narrowly define the ministerial roles allocated to women. It is our blessing to be able to teach biblical studies to students from all those traditions. Thus, it's not uncommon for me to have a female student with a deep conviction that she should only teach other females. While this is not my own position, I certainly want to honor her conviction. However, when I hear this conviction stated in a tone that suggests my female student feels she has a truncated or limited opportunity to serve, I like to point out that—as far as I know—about half the world is female. This (self-imposed) limitation still allows lots of opportunities to teach the Word. Whether or not you or your tradition restricts your circle of influence, for Bible scholars it is still a very, very large circle.

HELP ME SEE WHAT I MISS

Certainly, the world needs Bible scholars in all shapes and sizes. Yet, more than that, the very discipline of biblical studies needs voices from everywhere. The Great Tradition speaks from the past but still has insights for churches from different ages and settings. Likewise, our fellow believers, male and female, and from different cultures, supply us with fresh perspectives. Living in Indonesia helped me see how my Western upbringing had put blinders on me. I was reading the Bible through American glasses. Worse, I was reading them through white, male, protestant glasses. My Indonesian brothers and sisters taught me that Ephesians 6:1, "Children, obey your parents in the Lord," didn't have an expiration date. My tradition had implied that Paul's command expired at age 18. They also taught me that Paul's command for women to dress modestly (1 Tim 2:9) was about economic modesty and not sexual modesty.[3] If we are to read Scripture accurately, it is important to have voices from across the globe.

> As an African American Bible scholar I would like to encourage ministers of color to give serious consideration to biblical studies. You will not only enhance your understanding of the full biblical narrative, you will also find solid hermeneutic and historiographical perspectives to enrich your teaching and preaching. It is intensely practical.
>
> Terriel Byrd, Bible scholar

---

[3]For more information on this, see E. Randolph Richards and Brandon J. O'Brien, *Misreading Scripture with Western Eyes* (Downers Grove, IL: InterVarsity Press, 2012).

Recently I attended a panel discussion led by Margaret Mac-Donald regarding her book *The Power of Children*.[4] Margaret brought to light fascinating implications about the role of children in the early Christian church—ideas that had never occurred to me. Margaret helped me to see challenges faced by early Christians I had never noticed. A Christian slave woman brought to the Christian meetings not only her own children but the children of her master (for whom she was caregiving). This was dangerous for her but was a major way that the gospel spread. Paul speaks directly to women and children in the congregations. More importantly, Margaret helped me to see the subtle messages that Paul gives to these exploited people in his audience, offering hope through the gospel.

What I'm saying is, scholars like me need scholars like you. Therefore, we challenge you to allow your gender, culture, heritage, and background to guide you to the insights that others of us cannot or do not see.

Don't Give Up When I'm a Jerk

Lastly, though, we want to encourage you. Although wonderful scholars like Jarvis, Lynn, Bernie, or Kathy have broken ground for you, there are still many prejudices and barriers to overcome. Sometimes white male scholars like us can be jerks. (We may even have stated some things in this chapter in insensitive ways—forgive us.) In spite of sometimes being jerks, we still need you to help us.

---

[4]*The Power of Children: the Construction of Christian Families in the Greco-Roman World* (Waco: Baylor Press, 2014).

> I'm not saying life is harder for female
> scholars in the Christian academy, but it is!
>
> Michael Bird, New Testament scholar

Lynn offers this advice to a woman beginning biblical studies:

Courage and encouragement: these two terms sum up the necessary ingredients for a female scholar's success in the field of biblical studies. Courage is that inner mindset that takes risks, ignores naysayers, and resolutely looks ahead. The cloak of courage, however, has not been designed to fit comfortably on a woman's body. A Greek term for courage, *andreíos*, is based on the root word for "male." A Hebrew phrase to describe courage, "gird up your loins," hardly calls to mind a feminine act. The modern image of courage emphasizes physical strength, heroic risks of personal safety, and often situations of violence such as a battlefield. Despite these deterrents, a female biblical scholar can draw on biblical examples of courage that center on obedience to God's calling. Jesus laid down his life for his friends, and Mary, his mother, courageously stood with him as he did so.

Being courageous would be easier if your colleagues were role models of support and encouragement. Alas, it isn't always true. Kathy added this caution:

Let your words be accessible, compelling . . . and kind. It is important to be kind. In fact, beware lest the oppressed become the oppressor. As women scholars, we are tempted to develop gender-based chips on our shoulders—big ones. This consequence is extraordinarily unhelpful. Too often women shift the focus away from their contribution to the guild; obsession with "my rights" and "my oppression" is an egocentric dead-end that weakens the influence of all female academicians. If women want an equal voice, we must allow—and advocate—the same for all, even the over-stereotyped white male.

Courage tempered with grace. The church is not yet perfect, and it will not be easy. You will need thick skin to go with your tender heart. Great saints have gone before you, however, and plowed the ground. Thirty years ago, Marge and her husband Von were missionaries in Pakistan, Nepal, Bhutan, and India. Many of the national churches would not allow a woman to teach, even though Marge was the better Bible teacher—a fact that Von would readily admit. Usually within a few days, the nationals would realize this as well. Marge told me that many times she had to stand next to the lectern to teach (and not behind it where "official" teachers stood), and sometimes Von had to sit in the room, symbolically representing Marge was under his authority, I suppose. Nonetheless, this gracious woman saint (who I deeply admire) took these restrictions in stride. These were just some of many hardships she had to endure. Other hardships included being carried up mountains in a basket on the back of a Sherpa guide, being shipwrecked (figuratively) in a stalled automobile in a vast and empty Indian desert, stomach viruses, civil unrest, religious violence, and extended separation from family. The prejudices and discrimination against her as a female Bible teacher were undeserved and unfair. Marge rose above them. More than anyone else I know, she reminds me of the apostle Paul. There are now entire generations of ministers in those countries who have been educated at the feet of Marge. I can't help but smile at that thought. I have been blessed to know a true saint.

CONCLUSION: JOIN THE MOVEMENT

Kathy offers this word of advice:

> If it is to be an institution of integrity, the academy must offer equal opportunity to women and men. When we encounter the inverse, we must not stand by. I have found positive action to be more effective than persistent vocalization alone. Acceptance is not guaranteed, but to secure a place in evangelical academia, women must continue to act (and speak) competently with informed strength and grace. In short, my friends: do what you do, and do it well.

Thus we invite you, nay, *challenge* you, to join this noble calling with its honored history. Sure, the discipline deserves a black eye for ignoring, or worse, sidelining, voices from the margins, from black, brown, Hispanic and Asian ethnicities, and from women. Nonetheless, don't abandon the cause of basic biblical studies.

Make the sacrifices, do the hard work, earn your seat at the table. Be courageous and join the movement of biblical scholars.

9

STAY THE COURSE

■■■

HOW MUCH BIBLICAL TRAINING DO YOU NEED? The answer isn't simple; it depends on who's asking. Especially in America, we like to act as if everyone is the same. (Everyone is *equal*, but we are not the same.) Jesus himself said that some of us get one talent, some two and some five, "according to his ability" (Mt 25:15). Undergraduate seniors will occasionally ask me if I think they should continue to pursue graduate training in Bible. Graduate school is not for everyone, but I encourage them to continue with their education until the Lord says stop. Often the indication to stop is not a mysterious whisper in the night. Rather, the Lord can use a student's life situation, finances, or GPA to signal they have gone as far as they should at that moment.

There are lots of good reasons not to pursue advanced (or graduate) biblical training, but there are also a few poor reasons. Here are a few common but unreliable indicators that a student has gone as far in training as they need.

I'm tired of school. Every undergrad is tired by April of their senior year. That same person will visit me in August full of energy and wondering if it's too late to get into a graduate program. Just as college is very different from high school, so graduate school is not two more years of college. Most find the next tier of education to be so unlike the previous that they find the weariness is gone.

I've already learned all I need to know about the Bible. Although I am flattered that these students are satisfied with their degree, I tell them no matter how much they've learned there is still much more to learn (if the Lord has made them able). Most graduate programs go far deeper into a subject than undergraduate programs. My college course on Jesus tries to offer students a general understanding of the life and teachings of Jesus. But a graduate course on Jesus and the Gospels is not more of the same. We will analyze the independent themes and interconnectedness of the Gospels. We will explore the history of Jesus research to figure out how we have gotten to where we are so we can avoid repeating the same mistakes. Both programs have a course on Jesus, but the courses are not the same. In graduate school, you could take a semester course on just John 21. There is so much more to learn.

It's just a repeat. In graduate school (or seminary), you will learn new things, and, yes, you will also be reminded of some things you already know. This time you will process them more deeply. Just as you can never step into the same river again, a student never reads the same book again. I pored over St. Augustine's *Confessions* in one of my college courses. Years later I picked it up again and was amazed. What stood out to me in the *Confessions* as an unmarried college student no longer resonated with me as a married graduate student. Conversely, what was now resonating with me had not even been on my radar as an undergraduate. The book hadn't changed, but I had. How much more with studying the Bible! In fact, Augustine confessed that he had a similar experience with Scripture. The eighteen-year-old Augustine thought he already knew it all. He later confessed that he had been too puffed up with pride. He had come to realize that as he grew, the meaning of Scripture grew with him. Likewise, we encourage you to set aside pride. You may already be well versed in Scripture and have many valuable ministry experiences, but there is much to learn, even in returning to a plowed field. Who knows what new treasure you may unearth (Mt 13:44).

I'll just study on my own after I graduate. Well, we hope you will do that, but more than of a book or a lecture, we are a product of our teachers. We learn just as much from their character as from their words and just as much from informal conversations as from formal lectures. When we're in the classroom, it's sometimes the unplanned tangent or a seemingly random remark that God uses to make a life-changing impression. Just as two of John's disciples followed Jesus and wanted to know where he stayed so that they could imitate him in all things (Jn 1:35-38), perhaps you should continue to a divinity school or seminary, not just for a degree but for a mentor who is an expert in the Word. Even the ancient Stoic philosophers knew you needed mentors to help you regulate your characters since "you can never straighten that which is crooked unless you use a ruler."[5] Although there are many

---

[5]Lucius Annaeus Seneca, *Epistulae Morales* 1-65, trans. Richard M. Gummere, LCL 75 (Cambridge, MA: Harvard University Press, 1917–2004), 65.

places to find mentors who imitate Christ, seminaries and divinity schools are arguably some of the best places to do so. As we imitate the faithful lives of these leaders, our lives—by extension—become worthy of imitation.

There's nothing left to research. The Bible has been around for thousands of years. Everything has already been said. Any scholar writing before 1950 didn't have the Dead Sea Scrolls, which radically changed our thinking about a lot of the Old Testament. Every time an archaeologist sticks her shovel into the ground we could have our world reoriented. It's not just archaeologists uncovering buried treasures. Right now, a lot of scholars are arguing that we need to read the New Testament and Paul's letters in light of Jewish apocalyptic thought, which we are just now beginning to understand better. [6] A recent volume on Romans from some bright young scholars demonstrates how some of the insights from Jewish literature from the Second Temple period can help us understand Paul.[7] There is a lot of work to do there. Other young scholars, though, are still insisting that we aren't done mining the treasures of Greek and Roman culture.[8] What

---

[6]See *The Apocalyptic Tradition and the Shaping of New Testament Thought,* ed. Benjamin E. Reynolds and Loren T. Stuckenbruck (Minneapolis, MN: Fortress Press, forthcoming) and *Paul and the Apocalyptic Imagination,* ed. Benjamin Blackwell, John Goodrich, and Jason Maston (Minneapolis, MN: Fortress Press, 2016).

[7]*Reading Romans in Context,* ed. Benjamin Blackwell, John Goodrich, and Jason Maston (Grand Rapids: Zondervan, 2015).

[8]See, e.g., *Paul and the Greco-Roman Philosophical Tradition,* ed. Joseph R. Dodson and Andrew Pitts (London: LNTS, forthcoming). N. T. Wright notes, "Tracking, plotting and assessing the many lines and levels of his [Paul's] engagement with his complex *non-Jewish world* is a task awaiting further attention." *Paul and the Faithfulness of God* (Minneapolis, MN: Fortress Press, 2013), 2:1407. Italics ours.

else can be said about ancient Roman philosophy and the New Testament? Well, evidently quite a bit.[9]

Furthermore, John Barclay has recently stirred up the academy by calling into question our basic understanding of grace.[10] He suggests it doesn't mean what you and I think it means after all! This semester I (Randy) am in a group of scholars who meet on Thursday mornings to discuss this new book. The discussion is led by one of my former students, now a Bible scholar. This former student is completely changing how I understand Galatians and Romans. Another of the young men I taught to read Greek has become an expert on an aspect of ancient manuscripts. Now he's teaching me. Biblical scholarship is not something that one generation figures out so that young scholars have no more work to do. Rather, biblical scholars stand on the shoulders of their teachers. They can often see further as a result. Whether in a church Bible study or a classroom, new Bible scholars often point out fresh insights that we, their teachers, never saw.[11] To be sure, scholarship has brought us a long way, but the work isn't done. There are new treasures out there for you to uncover.

---

[9]See *Paul and Seneca in Dialogue*, ed. Joseph R. Dodson and David E. Briones (Leiden: Brill 2017). See also Troels Engberg-Pedersen, *Cosmology and Self in the Apostle Paul* (Oxford: Oxford University Press, 2010).

[10]John M. G. Barclay, *Paul and the Gift* (Grand Rapids: Eerdmans, 2015). See also David E. Briones, *Paul's Financial Policy* (London: Bloomsbury, 2014).

[11]See Scot McKnight, *The King Jesus Gospel* (Grand Rapids: Zondervan, 2011), 11.

PURSUE BIBLICAL STUDIES
FOR THE RIGHT REASON

It's possible to do the right thing for the wrong reason. Pursue biblical studies for the right reasons. First, do *not* make getting a job the ultimate reason for pursuing biblical studies. Although paying the bills and contributing to the family budget are certainly important, only some of you will use biblical studies in your primary vocation. Others of you will minister bivocationally or in volunteer positions. Consider biblical studies as a means to invest the talents God has given you rather than just a means to an occupation.

Second, a larger ministry isn't the right reason to pursue biblical studies. While in school, I (Randy) was invited to lead a youth retreat at a small country church. During that week I learned the pastor had graduate degrees in biblical studies. I was also surprised to learn he was quite smart and a gifted preacher. I didn't understand. He had been "stuck"—in my immature thinking—at this little church for over thirty years. I asked my professor who had arranged my invitation. As the pastor's confidante, he actually knew the pastor had been invited many, many times to pastor other (bigger) churches. He always refused, claiming God had not released him. My professor asked me, "Were the man's talents wasted, since he only had two dozen members?" I was thinking yes but kept my mouth shut. My professor gently reminded me that Jesus had few disciples and preached mostly in small villages. He then challenged me: "What if that man's obedience is a pleasing aroma to the Lord?" Degrees in biblical studies are not for the purpose of climbing some perceived ladder of ministry success.

If you believed us when we said it's important to have ministers who are scholars, then our churches need more minister-scholars. In school, I sat next to David Uth, who also finished his PhD in New Testament and has served in pastoral ministry ever since. Tens of thousands of Christians in Florida are fed every week from his faithful teaching of the Bible. Other minister-scholars use their advanced understanding of Scripture to write books and blogs and send out podcasts where complex teachings of the Bible are shared in compelling and understandable ways.

> In an essay Craig Blomberg writes,
>
>> What arguably could use some bolstering is the body of mid-level, semi-popular works, written by responsible scholars, often as an outgrowth of their own more technical work, to help bridge the gaps between the town and gown, church and seminary. Some might even consider a calling to this level of writing.[12]
>
> This short piece became instrumental in understanding my calling precisely to this level of writing. Blomberg's challenge shaped my entire ministry of writing and for that I'm thankful.
>
> J. Scott Duvall, New Testament scholar

---

[12]Craig Blomberg, "A Pathway in the Holy Scripture," in *Critical Issues in New Testament Studies for Evangelicals Today,* ed. Philip E. Satterthwaite and David F. Wright (Grand Rapids: Eerdmans, 1994), 51-79.

Finally, I would encourage you to look beyond the developed world. In the emerging world minister-scholars with all levels of training are often desperately needed. It's common to say we should be sending our best and brightest to the mission field. Do we really believe that? I spent nearly a decade traveling among isolated islands in the more remote regions of Indonesia. Friends would say, "Gracious, Randy, that's five miles past the Great Commission." I sometimes joked that while it wasn't the edge of the world, you could see it from there. Some would unkindly ask why someone with a PhD would be needed there. Well, wonderful Christians live there who deserve good Bible teaching as much as any other place. I trained Bible scholars there. Several of them advanced to doctoral degrees and are teachers in those locations. Six of the eight national leaders of an entire denomination are my former students. My efforts, though meager, weren't wasted. Some of you may plan to teach in the emerging world. What some may label as the margin, God might call the leading edge. Rather than enjoying the prestige of training the echelon in Jerusalem and being colleagues with the likes of Gamaliel, Jesus served alongside uneducated fishermen. If Jesus didn't consider the small villages in Galilee too remote for his biblical teaching, should we? Are you willing to be faithful to your vocation to teach even if it is in a location people consider insignificant?

Conclusion

This past summer I (Joey) was blessed with an amazing opportunity to speak at Clydehurst Christian Camp nestled in the breathtaking mountains of Montana. I used the occasion to take my thirteen-year-old son on his rite-of-manhood hike. The first day we went on a grueling and dangerous seven-hour climb that resulted in cuts, scrapes, bruises, tears, and even a little vomit. (It didn't help that halfway up, he conceded, "I really picked a bad day to go without underwear." Boys!) But my boy is tough. Every time I asked him if he wanted to quit, he would wipe the moisture from his eyes or the blood from his wound and refuse to stop. He continued placing one hand over the other. He knew there was still more to see. The strenuous effort paid off when we reached the summit. Such a view can only be seen from the top.

Likewise, God has perhaps given you the opportunity that few people have. While many Christians (we hope) will have the chance to study the Bible under a gifted Bible teacher in their church, a relatively small number will enjoy the blessing of biblical studies at the college or seminary level. If God has called you to this and has given you this opportunity, don't quit until you have reached your goal. To be sure, the trek will not be easy. It's a long journey that may evoke blood, tears, and vomit. There may even be chafing. You may experience the urge to quit early, and tempting offers will likely come along. Sometimes the temptation comes from another discipline or major that promises a bigger paycheck. We absolutely need Christian accountants and pharmacists, but woe to the Bible teacher who allowed herself to be diverted from her calling by promises of financial gain. Sometimes the temptation comes from a church. While in college, for example, you may serve so well as a part-time minister that they will offer you a full-time position. Obviously, you feel sufficiently trained for that position—you're currently doing it. But what of the future positions the Lord may have planned for you? Don't quit until you have fully multiplied the talents God has specifically given to you. Producing two talents was fine for the person given two talents. What if you have been given five? After all, the journey to be a Bible scholar is not a quick sprint on an indoor treadmill but a rigorous hike through misty mountains or a careful crawl through rare caverns. Stay the course.

CONCLUSION

Don't Miss the Forest for the Trees

■ ■ ■

THIS OLD PROVERB OF NOT MISSING the forest for the trees persists because there is truth in it. Sometimes we lose track of the big picture because we are looking at the details. For most of us, the deep study of Scripture is not our final goal. Most of us entered biblical studies to form a solid foundation for ministry.

SERVE IN MINISTRY

A student can usually tell the difference in professors who have served or are serving in some capacity as ministers. In Malachi 2:16, the Lord declares, "I hate divorce" (NRSV). One professor understands the Hebrew syntax and explains the ancient Near Eastern social background. Another professor knows all those things but has also ministered to a woman who has crumpled into her arms because of a looming divorce.

> Why are we engaging in scholarship in the first place?
> Is it not because we want to make a difference? . . .
> Jesus chose his disciples to bear fruit that would last
> (John 15:16). We want to have a lasting impact. How
> can we expect to have this kind of effect on the lives of
> others? . . . The key to lasting significance is for the
> scholar to seek to use research, writing, and teaching
> to advance the kingdom of God. In the end, nothing
> else will really matter.[1]
>
> Andreas J. Köstenberger, New Testament scholar

Likewise, members can spot a minister who really knows his
or her Bible well. In the *Republic*, Socrates dreamed of a society
where kings were philosophers and philosophers were kings. So
also the church needs scholars who are ministers and ministers
who are scholars. It's great to have the mind of a Bible scholar,
but to what avail if he or she does not also have the spirit of a
minister to complement it? Therefore, stretch yourself by keeping
one foot in the Ivory Tower and one foot in the church while you
keep your heart in both.

For those preparing in a college or seminary context, there is
an added danger: the ebb and flow of the academic calendar.
Students arrive in August amidst the whirl and chaos of the beginning of the academic year, often with weekend activities. Sud-
denly it's October. The student realizes he hasn't really been to
church. He visits a couple of churches. It's time to think about
getting planted in a particular church, but the student thinks, *It's
nearly Thanksgiving and I'll be heading home*. He returns, faces a

---

[1]Andreas J. Köstenberger, *Excellence* (Wheaton, IL: Crossway, 2011), 82-83.

blur of final exams, and Christmas looms. He justifies his slowness. *I'll join in the spring.* Yet the spring semester has a similar rhythm. The student seems to turn around twice and it's April. *Well, there's no use joining now, I'm heading home* or to camp or on a mission trip this summer. Sadly, many times I've encountered a biblical studies student nearing the end of his education who "never got around to joining a local church." Someone who says he will get involved in ministry after he finishes his biblical studies is unworthy to start in the first place.

USE YOUR TOOLS

Biblical studies is a tool in your ministry tool belt. It may even be one of your most important tools, but it is still just a tool— something you use in order to accomplish your task, your calling, your ministry. When my family and I lived in Indonesia, we wanted kitchen cabinets. We didn't want to stack our dishes on the floor. Wood workers lived on another island. The carpenter came (with his young helper) and moved into the carport next to my house. Every morning, they would start by sharpening their tools by hand. I watched a man sit on the ground, hold a handsaw with his feet and file each tooth of the saw with a small file. He worked one tooth after another down the four-foot blade of the handsaw. It took quite a while. Then he moved to the chisels. I fretted: there's only so much daylight and there was no working after the sun went down. But this old carpenter knew it actually saved time to take the time to prepare sharp tools. If you have not yet had the chance to use a handsaw, you might not understand this point. A sharp saw will glide through the task of cutting a board. A dull saw will take twice as long and three times the effort. Abraham Lincoln is often credited with the saying, "If I had five minutes to chop down a tree, I'd spend the first three sharpening the axe."[2]

But there is another danger, if we can stretch this metaphor a bit more. What if the carpenter spent all day working on his tools? What if he used the entire day to sharpen the saws, oil tools, cut and shape new handles for the hammers, and polish everything, and never got around to actually building any cabinets? The fair question to ask about such a carpenter would be What good is he? A similar charge is made—sometimes justly— against Bible scholars who hone their skills but never put them to work in the service of the church. We can become so engrossed in preparation that we never stop preparing. What a shame to spend so much time preparing to teach the Bible that we never actually get around to teaching the Bible. For some the Ivory Tower has a siren's call that's deadly. We don't crash on the rocks, but we never leave the Tower.

INVEST IN WHAT REALLY MATTERS

Work to become a Bible scholar in order that you may communicate the Bible in ways that change people's lives. Heaven will be full of people, not publications. One afternoon, I was laboring in my office. It was hot in the rainforest of Indonesia and I was sweating as I typed away. After I finished what I was working on, I pulled out an article I wanted to read from one of my folders. As I read I thought, *This is really good. I like this.* I glanced out my window and saw in the distance a group of students trudging

---

[2]The source is disputed; see quoteinvestigator.com/2014/03/29/sharp-axe.

> Karl Barth was undoubtedly one of the greatest theolo-
> gians of all time. But in 1962, speaking at Rockefeller
> Chapel at the University of Chicago, Barth was asked if
> he could summarize his whole life's work in a sentence.
> He answered simply, "Jesus loves me, this I know, for
> the Bible tells me so." I love this story and find it greatly
> encouraging. For all the complexity of Barth's writings
> and theology, he remained grounded in this simple
> truth: Jesus loves me. . . . Sometimes we biblical scholars
> get so caught up in the complexities and details of our
> work that we can easily forget what it is all about and
> why we are doing it.
>
> Constantine R. Campbell, New Testament scholar

down the road. Ours was the only house down there, so I knew
they were heading to see me. *Randy,* I thought to myself. *How
will you ever get anything done with all these interruptions?* I
sighed and flipped to the end to at least see who had written the
article. It was me. No wonder I liked it! The article had been
misfiled. At that moment the Lord spoke to me: If I didn't even
remember writing it, who really will remember reading it? Those
students are my legacy. They matter.

TAKE CARE OF YOUR HEART

Last and most important, a Bible scholar has to guard his or her
heart. We are not immune to the temptations that riddle the
church. We are just as vulnerable, if not more, to sins of selfish
ambition and sexual promiscuity. The lives of David and Solomon
should warn us of what happens when our hearts and minds no
longer follow after the Lord. Sin can disqualify new Bible scholars

before they even launch. They become as useless as the sprinter who jumps the gun. Don't lose the race before you start.[3]

> I am reminded often of the words of D. L. Moody: "If I take care of my character, my reputation will take care of itself."
>
> John Goodrich, New Testament scholar

There is another danger to the heart—more subtle, less spectacular than sensual sins but just as deadly. Biblical studies is the critical study of the Bible. We are quick to point out that *critical* means analytical not criticizing; nonetheless, we will teach you to break things down, analyze them, ponder them. We will teach you to question assumptions, and not to jump to conclusions. We will teach you to steer away from the ditch on the side of the road where one uncritically believes whatever is dished out. That's good. But in steering away from there, you don't want to veer all the way over and fall into the ditch on the other side, where you quit believing anything.

Let me illustrate by paraphrasing an old joke.[4] A Bible student, a Bible teacher, and a Bible scholar were on a train traveling

---

[3]We serve a God who delights in second chances. He lavishes forgiveness, but we should note that it is a *second* chance; the first one is gone. The sprinter may be allowed to compete in a different race, but the first race was lost.

[4]I am adapting an old joke that has likely been adapted many times previously. I first encountered it as a joke about an astronomer, a physicist, and a mathematician. See Ian Stewart, *Concepts of Modern Mathematics* (Mineola, NY: Dover Books, 1995), 286.

through Scotland. As they rounded the bend, they saw a small flock of black sheep up on the hillock. "Wow," exclaimed the Bible student. "*All* sheep in Scotland are black." The Bible teacher wisely seeks to help. "Perhaps," she cautions, "it might be better to say that *some* sheep in Scotland are black." The old Bible scholar then grouses, "At least on one side."

While it is technically accurate that only one side of the sheep could be seen at that moment, we don't want to become as skeptical as that Bible scholar. If you wait until 100 percent of your questions are answered before you believe, you might never believe. Some of you, as you study, will find it necessary to jettison some beliefs or doctrines you currently hold—you will discover they don't fit with Scripture. But don't jettison all of them. We are convinced that if your education doesn't change your mind about at least one thing, you should demand your money back. But we are equally convinced that your education should not undermine your basic faith. In a doctoral class one sleepy afternoon in 1987, my professor, W. D. Davies, quipped about H. J. Cadbury, the Hollis Professor of Divinity at Harvard (1934–1954) that he could "scarcely endure the weight of a single certainty." His studies had driven him to agnosticism. To me, nothing seems sadder than a Jesus scholar who is no longer a Jesus follower. As you guard your mind from a naive piety, guard also your heart from a hardened skepticism. As we noted in the introduction, studying about the Bible should never replace studying the Bible. In the opening lines of one of the greatest devotional books of all time, Thomas à Kempis wrote (ca. 1418–1427) this wise caution: "Indeed it is not learning that makes a man holy and just, but a virtuous life makes him pleasing to God. I would rather feel contrition than know how to define it."[5]

Likewise, we believe exegeting the Bible well will help you to experience the truth of Scripture more deeply and to teach it more effectively. But more importantly, we hope we have encouraged you to experience the truth of Scripture and not merely to exegete it.

SCUBA OR SNORKEL?

What kind of Bible scholar will you be? I was recently invited to teach Bible interpretation at Koza Baptist Church in Okinawa, Japan. When I accepted the offer, the pastor said he would like to take me scuba diving or snorkeling while I was there. He asked me which I preferred, and I told him I preferred to scuba dive. When the day came, however, the pastor found out that I did not have a scuba license. "Joey," he said, "you will have to settle for snorkeling." I was so disappointed. Because I had never taken the time to join a scuba course, I was bound to the surface. I didn't have the proper training or equipment to plunge into the depths of the sea. While gazing at the fish and the coral reef from the top, I could only imagine what I would have experienced in the deep. Randy, who has been diving since 1976, likes to taunt me: "Sure, a snorkeler at ten feet can enjoy the Great Barrier Reef (in a few places), but to *really* see the stunning fish and the gorgeous coral, you need to dive far deeper than a snorkel can take you."

---

[5]Thomas à Kempis, *The Imitation of Christ*, Dover Thrift Edition (Mineola, NY: Dover Books, 2003), 1.

We hope we have convinced you to take the time and effort to gain the training and tools to go deeper into God's Word. Most preachers and teachers learn sooner or later that you can only take the church as deep as you can go yourself. It's okay to splash around the surface, but you have to be willing to endure the training and don the equipment if you want to explore the depths. Take the plunge!

NAME AND SUBJECT INDEX

SCRIPTURE INDEX

LITTLE BOOKS SERIES

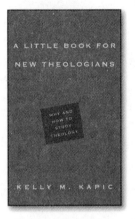

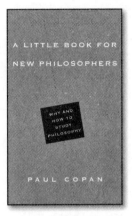

**A LITTLE BOOK FOR
NEW THEOLOGIANS**

Kelly M. Kapic

**A LITTLE BOOK FOR
NEW PHILOSOPHERS**

Paul Copan

**A LITTLE BOOK FOR
NEW SCIENTISTS**

Josh A. Reeves & Steve Donaldson

Finding the Textbook You Need

The IVP Academic Textbook Selector
is an online tool for instantly finding the IVP books
suitable for over 250 courses across 24 disciplines.

www.ivpress.com/academic/